AROUND THE WORLD WITH A GOURMET COOK

The best of the world's most famous foods can now be prepared in your own kitchen. Culinary expert Morrison Wood shows how readily available ingredients are transformed into exotic fare by the creative use of American wines and liqueurs.

The dishes of France, Spain, Italy, Germany, the East Indies and the Orient . . . the secrets of famous chefs . . . are combined in this unique cookbook.

Follow the simple, complete, step-by-step instructions; the result will be food to delight the most exacting gourmet, the most sophisticated palate.

The author has gathered his culinary knowledge from many countries. Along with the recipes he includes lively anecdotes about their origins, and how he happened to discover them.

Other SIGNET Titles You Will Enjoy

COOKING WITH WINE

by MORRISON WOOD

Formerly titled: SPECIALTY COOKING WITH WINE

A SIGNET BOOK from
NEW AMERICAN LIBRARY
TIMES MIRROR

APOLOGIA

This is not only a volume of gourmet cookery, but also a guidebook to exciting culinary adventures that make eating an alluring pleasure and cooking a festive event. It contains the most outstanding recipes from my first cookbook, *With a Jug of Wine* (which is one of the best-selling specialty cookbooks in America, now in its 19th printing), and the companion volume, *More Recipes With a Jug of Wine.*

If you are looking for recipes such as Miss Sally Arbuthnot's celebrated (in Round Corners, Nebraska) corn chowder, or Aunt Samantha's escalloped tuna fish, or the chocolate meringue pie that won first prize at the Sulpha County Fair, don't waste your time going any further.

However, if you are seeking new taste thrills; if you'd like to become a renowned host or hostess; if you'd like to cook your way into a man's (or woman's) heart; or if you have an adventuresome spirit and yearn to experiment, or try something new in the way of gourmet food, you've bought yourself a piece of goods!

The term "gourmet," in connection with individuals, food, and cooking, is misinterpreted by a great many people, who look upon a gourmet as a food snob addicted to showy extravagance; upon gourmet food as rare, exotic, and expensive; and upon gourmet cooking as the preparation of superfancy food in the grand manner, accompanied by rich and complicated sauces.

Nothing could be further from the truth. In my lexicon a gourmet is an ordinary individual with taste and intelligence who is fond of good food, and eats it to delight his palate rather than to keep himself alive. He doesn't scorn plain fare as long as it is appetizingly prepared, but he prefers unusual dishes that have taste-teasing flavors. He may sit down to a perfectly appointed table and be served dishes so delectable that their preparation requires great skill. Or he may sit down at the kitchen table and, from plastic plates, eat a humble beef stew that he or his wife has prepared. In either case, if he realizes that the food before him is not only nourishment for his body, but also a pleasure to his palate, and appreciates its ingeniously contrived variations, he is a gourmet. Gourmet food is any food, not necessarily expensive, which has an unusual and delicious flavor due to the imaginative combinations of ingredients and seasonings. It might be lamb shanks, chicken fricassee, hamburgers, or a pot roast of beef, as well as Tournedos of Beef Rossini, Frogs' Legs Provençale, or Filet of Sole Marguery.

Gourmet cooking is not an art known only to arduously trained, highly skilled professional chefs. In order to practice it one does not have to be a "born" cook, or a graduate of a cooking school. It doesn't require an ultramodern kitchen with a large collection of fancy utensils and gadgets. It does not necessarily call for uncommon foodstuffs, expensive cuts of meat, or a wide variety of vintage wines. It does call for, on the part of a cook, a love of good food, some imagination, and a willingness to experiment.

Quite simply, gourmet cooking is taking advantage of the tremendous variety of the food possibilities that nature offers, and combining them to produce new combinations of delicious flavors, aided and abetted by the judicious use of herbs and wines, which are merely flavoring agents.

Traditionally, we Americans are apt to look upon wine as a luxury. Yet the humblest European peasants (the thriftiest people in the world) use wine as matter-of-factly as we use butter or sugar. Of course, they use what they call the wine of the country, or *vin ordinaire*, which is very cheap. Very well, so can Americans use the wine of their country which, with a few exceptions, equals or surpasses the ordinary wines of European countries.

Flavor is called the soul of food. It is flavor that makes all dishes—hot or cold, sweet or sour—enjoyable. And wine adds an indefinable flavor to a great many foods. As a matter of fact, wine and food are sweethearts!

Once again I would like to correct the erroneous impression that wine or liquor is employed in cooking for its alcoholic content. With the few exceptions where spirits are used as a last-minute flavoring, the alcohol contained in the bottled ingredients will have evaporated long before the dish is served. For instance, it is perfectly safe to serve fruits cooked or baked in wine to children, or to Aunt Mehitabel, president of the local W. C. T. U. What little alcohol there was will all be gone, but a heavenly flavor will have permeated an otherwise dull fruit. The same thing applies to meat, poultry, fish, and game cooked with wine or spirits; or, for that matter, to a Soufflé Grand Marnier. If little Johnny and teen-aged Mary Lou are allowed to have a bit of that soufflé, the Grand Marnier flavor won't hurt them any more than would the customary few drops of vanilla extract, which, by the way, contains a fairly large percentage of alcohol.

As I said in the beginning, this is a volume containing outstanding recipes for gourmet food. Whether you're a neophyte or an old kitchen hand, you will have no trouble in following the recipes. If you can read the English language, if you can count up to twenty—with or without taking off your shoes—and if you can follow explicit directions, you can make any dish detailed in this book, and do it well. Just recently a letter came to me from a woman who had given my first book to her newly married niece. "She literally could not boil an egg correctly," the woman wrote, "but she is now becoming a gourmet cook—wines and all!"

Many of the recipes contained herein have appeared in my syndicated weekly cooking column, "For Men

Only!" over the past dozen years. They are tried, tested, and true. Through the years my rather large volume of mail from bankers, industrialists, businessmen, mechanics, ministers, housewives, secretaries, and businesswomen have been filled with praise for the recipes they have tried and have found to be "out of this world!"

Why have I written my cookbooks? I believe there are many women and a great number of amateur male cooks who would like to have a cookbook that omits the ordinary, run-of-the-mill recipes, and the very difficult recipes, and presents unusual and delectable recipes that they can prepare and cook.

In other words, ladies and gentlemen, here is something upon which you can build reputation and fame. In some cases your friends may have misgivings as they sit down to your table to partake of a meal you have prepared. But believe me, they'll applaud when the meal is over. For the husband, when the Little Woman has gone home to Mother, either for a vacation or for a salutary effect, it won't be necessary to eat out of cans, in expensive restaurants, or at Ptomaine Pete's lunch counter. For the ladies, they can often make the approach to a new hat, an Easter outfit, or a new fur coat much less painless by serving their so-called "better half" with a superlative dish. That old saw, "The way to a man's heart is through his stomach," can be amended to: "The way to a man's pocketbook is through a satisfied tummy."

Finally, for bachelors, cooking offers a new and better approach than that timeworn gag, "How would you like to come up and see my etchings?"

Morrison Wood

COOKING
WITH WINE

CONTENTS

4 FISH 60

5 SHELLFISH 71

6 MEAT 90

7   *GAME*   *128*

1. WINE

God made Man, frail as a bubble
God made Love, Love made Trouble
God made the Vine; was it a sin
That Man made Wine to drown Trouble in?

Oliver Herford

Wine is a simple, natural, and delightful thing. As the Psalmist said, "it maketh glad the heart of man." And long before, Plato, the great Greek philosopher, wrote: "Nothing more excellent or valuable than wines was ever granted by the gods to man."

In this chapter I should like to tell you very simply about wine, how to select it, how to serve it, and how to enjoy it. And I'm going to talk about American wines, not only because they are excellent and enjoyable and reasonably priced, but because they avoid many of the complexities of European wines.

Getting acquainted with wine does not involve an extensive knowledge of viticulture and grapes, nor a strict adherence to the rituals of tasting and serving. Which wine goes best with what food is easily and quickly learned, and you can forget most of the dogmatic statements you have heard or read about. You can also dismiss, but quickly, all the snobbery and semantics with which a few so-called sophisticates and phony connoisseurs have surrounded the whole subject of buying, serving, and drinking wine.

The two most important things to know about wine are the *classes* and *types* of wine. Virtually all wines fit into five classes: appetizer wines, red table wines, white table wines, sweet dessert wines, and sparkling wines.

APPETIZER WINES:

These are so-called because they are favored for before-meal or cocktail use, and in America largely consist of sherry and vermouth. They both range from dry (not in the sense of sour, but rather in the sense of the opposite of sweet), to semi-sweet.

Sherry is characterized by its "nutty" flavor, and ranges in color from pale to dark amber. It may be dry (so labeled), or medium (sometimes labeled "cocktail sherry"), or sweet (sometimes labeled "cream sherry"). The alcoholic content of sherries is around 20 per cent. Sherry may or may not be served chilled.

Vermouth is wine flavored with herbs and other aromatic substances. There are two types of vermouth—dry (French type) and sweet (Italian type). Their alcoholic content runs between 15 per cent and 20 per cent. Vermouth, according to the taste of many, is at its best when served chilled, or "on the rocks."

RED TABLE WINES:

These are usually dry, and accompany main-course dishes. There are two types, Burgundy and claret, and they both rarely exceed an alcoholic content of 12 per cent. They should be served at room temperature, or slightly below. It is often a good idea to draw the cork from the bottle about a half-hour before serving, to allow the wine a chance to breathe.

Burgundy-type table wines should be completely dry, full-bodied, rich in flavor and aroma, and deep red in color.

Claret-type table wines should be completely dry, light- or medium-bodied, with a fruity taste and aroma.

Rather a newcomer in America is a third type of red

wine called Rosé. This is literally a rose-colored wine, with a delicate grape sweetness without being sweet. It is light-bodied, fragrant, and fruity, and goes pleasantly with any food with which wine can be drunk. It should be served chilled.

WHITE TABLE WINES:

These vary from extremely dry and rather tart to sweet and full-bodied, and their delicate flavor blends best with white meats, fowl, and seafood. Their colors range from pale straw to gold. They should always be served chilled. Their alcoholic content is the same as red table wines. There are three types of white table wines: sauterne, Rhine, and white Burgundy.

While true French sauternes are white wines on the sweet side only, in America there are three kinds of sauterne; dry, medium, and sweet. The latter may be labeled "Haute" or "Château" sauterne. Sweet sauternes go best with desserts.

German white table wines vary from sweet to dry. But in America, Rhine wines are thoroughly dry, rather tart, and light-bodied, and of pale gold color.

The American white Burgunday table wines are similar to the white Burgundy wines of France. They are delicate, straw-colored, and less tart than the Rhine wines, with a more fruity flavor and heavier body.

DESSERT WINES:

These are sweet, full-bodied wines served with desserts, and as refreshments in the afternoon and evening. Their alcoholic content is usually around 20 per cent. The four types are port, white port, muscatel, and Tokay, with some other variations.

SPARKLING WINES:

The two most popular types are champagne and sparkling Burgundy, both of which are effervescent.

Champagne may be either straw-colored, pink, or red. It ranges from completely dry (usually labeled "Brut"), semi-dry (labeled "Extra Dry," "Dry," or "Sec"), and sweet (usually labeled "Doux"). Champagne may be served before dinner, with or without appetizers; with almost any dinner entree; and with dessert, always chilled.

Sparkling Burgundy is red, full-bodied, and moderately dry. It goes best with red meats and game, and is always chilled.

Wine type names are of two origins. Names like Burgundy, claret (the British name for red Bordeaux table wines), sauterne, Rhine, Chablis and champagne came into use centuries ago as the names of the wines of the Old World viticultural districts which were famous for those particular types of wines. As the wine types became known all over the world, the same names were applied to all wines, wherever grown, which had similar type characteristics. Such names are called *generic* names of geographical origin.

The other wine type name is *varietal,* and a wine is called a varietal wine when the wine type is named for the principal grape variety from which the wine is made. Such names as Cabernet, Pinot Noir, Gamay, Riesling, Semillon, Pinot Blanc, and Traminer are varietal names.

However, most of the varietal wines fall within one of the generic categories mentioned before. Thus, Cabernet and Zinfandel are both claret types, but with the special flavors and aromas of the cabernet and zinfandel grapes. Johannisberg Riesling, Grey Riesling, Sylvaner, and Traminer are really Rhine wines, broadly speaking. Pinot Blanc, Pinot Chardonnay and Folle Blanche are white Burgundy types. Semillon and Sauvignon Blanc are sauterne types.

In the eastern United States there are a number of varietal wines named after native American grapes, such as Isabella, Ives, and Norton (red wines), and Diamond, Diana, Dutchess, and Iona (white wines).

It is generally conceded that the best American wines have varietal names, an important buying point.

At this point it is possible, particularly if you are a novice, that you are slightly confused by the discussion of generic and varietal names. So, for clarity's sake, the following is a list of the principal red and white American table wines, and will indicate what wine name they have, from which locality they come, and their general characteristics. Copy this list if you will, and when you go shopping for wine, take the list with you and refer to it. You'll have as good, and possibly a better knowledge of American wines than the average dealer. Incidentally, the wine names preceded by an asterisk are, in my opinion, the very best American wines.

RED TABLE WINES

BARBERA: Italian type. Varietal. California. Full-bodied, robust, and fruity. Excellent with Italian food.

BURGUNDY: Burgundy type. Generic. California, Ohio, and New York. Quality varies. Better select a varietal type of Burgundy, such as a Pinot Noir. Goes with red meats, game, and cheese.

*CABERNET, or CABERNET SAUVIGNON: Claret type. Varietal. California. A superior quality wine, medium-bodied, rich, and fruity, with a soft fragrance. For red and white meats and fowl.

CHARBONO: Italian type. Varietal. California. Similar to Barbera, but inferior. Goes with Italian meals.

CHIANTI: Italian type. Generic. California and East. Pleasant, but not made from the same grapes as Italian Chianti. Medium-bodied, dry, fruity, and slightly tart. Goes with Italian foods.

CLARET: Claret (or Bordeaux) type. Generic. California and New York. Medium-bodied, soft, and fruity. Not as good as a Cabernet or Cabernet Sauvignon. Goes with red meats and fowl.

CRACKLING ROSÉ: A California Rosé containing a lively effervescence created through fermentation in the bottle. A delicious new concept. Serve chilled. All foods.

*GAMAY: Burgundy type. Varietal. California. Full-bodied and soft, with a fragrant bouquet. Excellent with red meats and cheese.

GAMAY ROSÉ: Rosé type. Varietal. California. Light

rose wine made from Gamay grapes. For all foods. Serve chilled.

*GRENACHE ROSÉ: Rosé type. Varietal. California. This wine is made from the Grenache grapes, which give it a superiority over the Gamay Rosé. Has a fruity fragrance. For all foods. Serve chilled.

GRIGNOLINO: Italian type. Varietal. California. Less robust than Barbera, but more tart. A pleasant wine with red meats and Italian food.

MOURESTAL: Claret type. Varietal. California. A wine with medium body, but on the thin side. Soft, with fruity aroma. Goes with red meats or fowl.

*PINOT NOIR: Burgundy type. Varietal. California. The finest of American Burgundy-type wines. Full-bodied, robust, with a fine bouquet and flavor. Serve with red meats, game and cheese.

RED PINOT: (See Pinot Noir.)

ROSÉ: Rosé type. California. A rose-colored wine, light-bodied and fruity. Goes with any food. Serve chilled.

VIN ROSÉ: (See Rosé, Gamay Rosé, and Grenache Rosé, and Crackling Rosé.)

*ZINFANDEL: Claret type. Varietal. California. A fairly light-bodied, tart, aromatic wine, with a fruity bouquet. A delightful luncheon or dinner wine. In this wine, look for the locality in California in which it is produced. The best comes from Sonoma and Napa counties, and the Santa Cruz Mountains. Serve with red meats and fowl.

WHITE TABLE WINES

CHABLIS: White Burgundy type. Generic. California and New York. A light, clean wine, with a somewhat flinty taste and fruity flavor. Pale amber color. Seldom a great wine outside France. Choose rather a varietal white Burgundy type, such as a Pinot Blanc or a Pinot Chardonnay. Serve chilled with seafoods, white meats, and fowl. Particularly good with oysters.

*DELAWARE: Rhine wine type. Varietal. New York and Ohio. Clean, fresh, and fruity, with a spicy bouquet.

New York wines of this type are drier, resembling a German Moselle. Serve chilled with seafood and fowl.

*DIANA: Rhine wine type. Varietal. New York and Ohio. A very dry clean wine on the astringent side, with a fresh and pleasing bouquet. Excellent with fish. Chill.

*DUTCHESS: Rhine wine type. Varietal. New York. Very dry and light, and slightly tart. Serve chilled with seafood and fowl.

DRY SAUTERNE: Sauterne type. Generic. California, Ohio, and New York. Great French sauternes are never dry, they vary only in sweetness. Most American "dry sauternes" are merely a white table wine with little character. Choose rather a dry Semillon or a Sauvignon Blanc.

*DRY SEMILLON: Sauterne type. Varietal. California. Along with Sauvignon Blanc, the very best of the "dry" sauternes. Fruity and medium full-bodied. An ideal main dinner wine with chicken, seafood, and white meats. Chill.

EMERALD DRY: Rhine type. Varietal. California. Made from new hybrid grape called Emerald Riesling. Resembles a fine German Moselle or Saar wine. Has a clean, subtle dryness together with a delicate, flowery bouquet. Serve chilled with seafood, poultry, light entrees.

FOLLE BLANCHE: White Burgundy type. Varietal. California. A delicate, dry, straw-colored wine, very refreshing. It is rather thin-bodied, with a slight acidity and flinty taste, similar to a French Chablis. Serve chilled with seafood and fowl.

*GEWURZTRAMINER: Rhine or Alsatian type. Varietal. California. Fragrant, distinctly aromatic with a spicy scent and flavor. So far, the outstanding Gewurztraminer is produced by Louis Martini. Serve chilled.

*GREY RIESLING: Rhine wine type. Varietal. California. This is not a true Riesling wine, but it is soft, mild, and refreshing, light in body and sprightly in character. Serve chilled with seafood, fowl, and light entrees.

HAUTE SAUTERNE: Sauterne type. Generic. California, Ohio, and New York. This name is usually applied to American sauternes which are sweeter than dry sauternes. A dessert wine.

*JOHANNISBERG RIESLING: Rhine wine type.

Varietal. California. One of the finest white wines of California. Sprightly, brilliant, fragrant, and fruity. It is excellent with all kinds of seafood and fowl. The best comes from the northern counties of California—Napa, Sonoma, and Santa Clara. Serve chilled.

MOSELLE: Rhine wine type. Generic. California. These are, as a rule, indifferent wines, and bear not the slightest resemblance to the German Moselles. Serve chilled with seafood and fowl.

*PINOT BLANC: White Burgundy type. Varietal. California. A superior wine, fresh, fragrant, quite lively in taste, and dry. Best with seafood and chicken, chilled.

*PINOT CHARDONNAY: White Burgundy type. Varietal. California. Another of the finest California wines, but scarce. Delicately fragrant, aromatic, rich in body. Excellent, chilled, with seafood and chicken.

RHINE: Rhine wine type. Generic. California, New York, and Ohio. Usually undistinguished in America, and often made from table grapes. For those wanting a wine comparable to the fine German Rhine wines, or Alsatian wines, a Johannisberg Riesling, a Sylvaner, a Traminer, or a Gewurztraminer should be selected.

RIESLING: Rhine wine type. Generic. California, New York, and Ohio. A dry, fresh, clean wine, very good if made from the riesling grape. But little of it really is. Better buy the Grey Riesling or Johannisberg Riesling. Serve chilled with seafood and fowl.

SAUTERNE: Sauterne type. Generic. California, Ohio, and New York. Wines so labeled can be made from almost any grape. Ohio, however, produces a delicate, semi-sweet sauterne labeled "Isle St. George," which is delightful. Serve chilled.

*SAUVIGNON BLANC: Sauterne type. Varietal. California. A fruity wine of extreme dryness, full-bodied, and of superb quality. Excellent with almost any meal, but best with shellfish and fowl. There is also a semi-sweet Sauvignon Blanc. The semi-sweet goes with chicken, and the sweet with desserts. Serve chilled.

*SWEET SEMILLON: Sauterne type. Varietal. California. A rich, full-bodied sauterne, fairly sweet. It is a wine to serve chilled, with desserts, and is wonderful in punches and cups.

SYLVANER: Rhine wine type. Varietal. California. This is more of an Alsatian wine than a Rhine. It is light, fresh, soft, and a little tart. Goes particularly well with seafood. Serve chilled.

*TRAMINER: Rhine (or Alsatian) type. Varietal. California. A fine dry wine of fragrant bouquet and flowery flavor. Some experts have called the Charles Krug Traminer California's finest white wine. Serve chilled with chicken, seafoods, and veal.

WHITE PINOT: White Burgundy type. Varietal. California. This name is sometimes used instead of Pinot Blanc, but in California the White Pinot wine is generally made from the Chenin Blanc grape, and should not be confused with the Pinot Blanc. It is pleasing, dry, light, and fruity. Serve chilled with seafood and fowl and light meats.

The prices of the foregoing varietal wines may run anywhere from a little more than a dollar a bottle (fifth) to two dollars a bottle, with two or three running up to nearly three dollars a bottle. I would say that the average would be about $1.45 per fifth. The generic wines are priced below the varietal wines, and in many cases may be purchased well under a dollar per fifth, and even cheaper if bought by the half gallon or gallon.

A new type of wine has recently made its appearance on the market. It comes from California, and is called an old-fashioned table wine. It is on the dry side, "Mellow," as one vintner puts it. They are in no sense premium-quality wines, and connoisseurs would wrinkle their noses in disdain at them. But they are very pleasant, especially for everyday drinking, and their price puts them within the reach of almost everyone. They sell for from ninety-six to ninety-nine cents a half gallon. I believe there are twenty-three California wine producers who bottle these wines, such as the Gallo Wine Company, under the label "Vino Paisano," the Petri Wine Company under the label "Marca Petri," and the Wine Growers Guild under the label "Vino da Tavola." For budget-wise families who enjoy wine with their meals, these wines are decidedly worth a trial.

There are a number of large wine companies which bottle wines which sell for around fifty to seventy-five cents a fifth. These are almost exclusively generic wines, and they are just ordinary. Some of these large companies also bottle premium wines, notably Cresta Blanca and Italian Swiss Colony.

Champagnes are bottled in many sections of the country, but in my opinion, and in the opinion of many others, the finest American champagnes have come from New York State. They are excellent, and have been superior to all but the great French champagnes. The two leading New York brands are Gold Seal, bottled by the Urbana Wine Company, of Hammondsport, New York, and Great Western, bottled by the Pleasant Valley Wine Company of Rheims, New York.

In the past year or so, however, a new group have taken over the F. Korbel & Brothers winery in northern California, which produces only sparkling wines. For many years Korbel champagne was probably the leading California champagne, but it did not come up to the New York State champagne. But since the Hecks have taken over, Korbel champagne now ranks as one of America's finest champagnes. I had some undosaged (unsweetened) Korbel champagne in September at the winery, and it was one of the finest champagnes I have ever drunk.

Another excellent California champagne, which is unique, is the Paul Masson Triple Red Champagne. This is not a pink champagne, nor a sparkling Burgundy, but a true champagne, with a red color.

In the field of vermouths, I must confess that I cannot enthuse over American dry vermouths. Many people consider Tribuno dry vermouth the best. But for a straight dry vermouth, or for a dry vermouth in mixing martinis, pay a dollar or so more and get Noilly Prat. On the other hand, I have tasted some excellent American sweet vermouths, both by themselves, chilled, and in cocktails. Tribuno also makes an excellent sweet vermouth.

I guess there is hardly a vintner in America who does not produce and bottle sherries. They range from excellent to pretty bad, and in price from around fifty cents a fifth to nearly $3.75 a fifth. I would say that the average price of an American premium-quality sherry would be about $1.50 a fifth.

As with sherry, scores of vintners throughout the United States produce and bottle dessert wines. And they too range from excellent to pretty dreadful. There are a number of fine American ports, notably those bottled by H. T. Dewey and Sons, of Egg Harbor, New Jersey, and the ports of Ficklin Vineyard, in California. Premium-quality ports average about the same price as sherries.

Most of the American muscatels and Tokays are very ordinary. The so-called Tokay wines in America do not even remotely resemble the Hungarian Tokays. However, there is a muscatel wine produced and bottled by Beaulieu Vineyards in California that is a fine, delicate after-dinner wine. It is labeled Muscat de Frontignan.

In buying American wines, there are three things to look for on a bottle's label: the varietal or generic name of the wine, the district in which the wine is made, and the vintner's name.

There are three principal districts in the United States which produce fine wines: California, Ohio, and New York State. In California, there are three localities which lie close to San Francisco that have a cool climate, which is favorable to slow-ripening grapes, and so produce the best red and white table wines. They are the Sonoma and Napa valleys, the Livermore-Contra Costa area, and the Santa Clara-Santa Cruz district. The San Joaquin Valley produces the finest dessert wines. Southern California, in the area northeast of Los Angeles, largely produces sweet wines.

In Ohio, the best wine-producing area is the Sandusky-Lake Erie Islands in the northern part of the state.

The Finger Lakes region in west-central New York State is considered to be the most important wine-producing area in the United States outside of California.

I wouldn't hazard a guess as to the number of wine producers there are in the United States. The following

list is by no means complete. There are many wineries
which produce and bottle fine wines, but who do not have
sufficient gallonage to warrant national distribution, and
the sale of their wines is indigenous to their location.
The vintners and companies I am listing, however, are
sound and reliable. Most of them have fairly wide distribution, and their name on a bottle of wine is indicative
of premium quality.

CALIFORNIA

Almaden Vineyards
Beaulieu Vineyards
Beringer Brothers
Buena Vista Vineyards
Christian Brothers
Concannon Vineyard
Cresta Blanca Wine Company
Ficklin Vineyards (notably port)
Inglenook Vineyard Company
Italian Swiss Colony (Asti Brand)
F. Korbel & Brothers (Champagne)
Charles Krug Winery
Paul Masson Vineyards
Louis M. Martini Winery
Novitiate of Los Gatos
Wente Brothers

NEW JERSEY

H. T. Dewey & Sons (notably port)

NEW YORK

Pleasant Valley Wine Company
Taylor Wine Company
Urbana Wine Company
Widmer's Wine Cellars

OHIO

Meier's Wine Cellars

Opinions on which wine should accompany each particular dish range from the sublime to the ridiculous. The
purist will say that white wine should never be served

with red meats or game, and that red wines should never be served with seafood. He believes that Chablis is the only wine that should be served with oysters. He will tell you, if you are going to serve wine, to abjure all dishes cooked in red wine, all rich, brown gravies, all sauces that contain wine or a preponderance of spices and herbs, and he will warn you that wine does not go well with eggs, tomatoes, carrots, and so on, ad infinitum.

On the other hand there are those who say with great gusto, "Forget any hard and fast rules. If you like a wine, drink it with anything." But the matter isn't quite that simple, and such advice is just as deadly as that of the purist. You would enjoy neither the wine nor the food if you drank a sweet sauterne with a steak, or a heavy Burgundy with a filet of sole. A good dish can easily be spoiled by drinking the wrong wine with it, just as an excellent wine can be disappointing when served with the wrong dish.

In general, the heavier-bodied red table wines go best with red meats, game, and cheese. The lighter red table wines can be served with fowl, and some of the more robust seafoods, as well as with red meats. Dry white table wines go best with white meats, fowl, and seafood, but also go well with lamb, veal, ham, and some of the variety meats. This is particularly true of the heavier-bodied dry white wines, such as the white Burgundy types. Sweet white wines should accompany deserts. Rosé wines can go with almost any food, as can champagne. And remember, white table wines, Rosé wines, champagne, and sparkling Burgundy should be served chilled. Red table wines should be served at room temperature, or a little below. *Apéritif* wines may be served at room temperature, or chilled. Dessert wines (outside of the sweet white wines) should be served at room temperature.

Forget all the nonsense about each type of wine needing its special glass. Your *apéritif* wines, sherry and vermouth, can be served in cocktail glasses, or, if served "on the rocks," in old-fashioned glasses. Table wines are usually served in five- to six-ounce stemmed glasses, about 5¾ inches high, and about 2¾ inches wide, tulip-shaped. You can get nice-looking, serviceable wineglasses in many liquor stores for about forty cents each. Of course, lovely crystal glassware adds eye appeal to the wine, and if you have such, use it by all means. Oh, yes, when serving wine, only fill the glasses about two-thirds full.

Wines keep best in dry, dark places, free from vibration, and at a temperature of 55 to 60 degrees Fahrenheit. If you have a basement, wonderful. If you live in an apartment, a closet will do very nicely, if it remains cool. You can make your own wine racks, or you can buy metal ones very reasonably, each holding twelve bottles. Of course, bottles should be stored on their sides, so that the corks will be kept moist, and no air will get in the bottle. In storing wine, keep white wines and champagne on the lowest levels, and red wines above them. Appetizer and dessert wines can be stored upright.

Finally, don't forget that, although wine is usually served without mixing, it is equally versatile in mixed cold drinks for summer, hot drinks for winter, punches and cups for parties all the year around, and cocktails anytime.

LIQUEURS

Liqueurs, or cordials, are very lovely things to look at, to sip slowly with your coffee after an excellent dinner, to use in cooking, or to use with ice creams. As a rule, they are expensive, but due to the fact that they are served and used in small portions, their cost is really not so high. And they do wonders for not only your taste buds, but your morale.

There are probably a hundred or more cordials on the market today, but some of them are special concoctions of some manufacturer and are known only in the locality where they are prepared. I should guess that there are about sixty really fine cordials, but many of these are unobtainable in the United States.

Cordials fall into two broad classifications: fruit cordials and plant cordials. It is said that some cordials, such as green chartreuse, contain up to 250 ingredients.

There is one cordial, Calisay, made in Spain, which is composed of more than 125 different herbs, plants and fruits.

A cordial is an artificial liquor or spirit prepared by one of two methods—maceration or infusion. In the first method, fruits and plants are steeped in brandy, or rectified spirit, for about six to eight months. Then other ingredients are added. In the second method, alcohol is mixed with the juices of fresh crushed fruit, then spiced and sweetened. Or alcohol is mixed with the oils of various plants, diluted with water, sweetened with sugar, and finally filtered. The best cordials are prepared by the maceration method.

APRICOT BRANDY or ABRICOTINE
This is an apricot cordial or brandy made from small French apricots.

ABSINTHE
The true absinthe is impossible to obtain today. Originally it contained wormwood, which is claimed to be a narcotic. If you are old enough, you will remember Madame X, in the famous play of that name, who had become an absinthe fiend. One of the finest pick-me-ups used to be an absinthe frappe. Today absinthe can be obtained sans wormwood under such trade names as Herbsaint or Pernod, both of which are still wonderful flavoring agents.

ANISETTE
This is compounded from anise-seed oil and oil of bitter almonds, dissolved in strong spirits.

BENEDICTINE
This is made from a large variety of herbs and good cognac brandy. It was originated by a Benedictine monk in Fécamp, France, over four hundred years ago and is still made in the same town.

The initials D.O.M. on the label stand for *Deo Optimo*

Maximo—To God, most good, most great.—the motto
of the Benedictine Order.

CHARTREUSE, GREEN or YELLOW
This cordial is made in Tarragona, Spain, although it
was originally made in France over three hundred years
ago. The recipe is a secret of the Carthusian Fathers.
The yellow chartreuse, made from 120 ingredients, is
86 proof and the green, prepared from about 250 ingredients, is 110 proof. These are two of the finest
liqueurs obtainable.

CHERRY HEERING
This cordial is made in Copenhagen, Denmark, from
fresh cherries, spice, sugar, and brandy.

COINTREAU
Cointreau, white curaçao, and triple *sec* are very similar, but Cointreau is sweeter than the other two. They
are all prepared from fine brandy, with orange peel as
their principal base. This is one of the ingredients of
the famous sidecar cocktail.

CRÈME DE CACAO
This cordial is prepared from cacao beans and fine
brandy. In a cordial glass, with cream floating on the
top, it is a favorite after-dinner drink of the gentler sex.
It is also the base of the Alexander cocktail, which is
another favorite with women.

CRÈME DE CASSIS
This cordial is made from black currants steeped in
fine brandy and sweetened with syrup. One of the best
known *aperitifs* in France is a *cassis vermouth,* which
is made with equal parts of crème de cassis, dry vermouth, and sparkling water added. This is a deliciously
cooling summer drink.

CRÈME DE MENTHE
This is prepared with cognac and fresh peppermint
leaves. It may be white or green. White crème de

menthe and brandy make up the well-known stinger cocktail.

CRÈME DE NOYAU

This cordial is primarily used as a flavor in mixed drinks. It is compounded from brandy, bitter almonds, nutmeg, mace, and the kernels of apricot or peach pits.

CRÈME DE ROSE

This is made from aromatic seeds and brandy, and sweetened with rose petals. It is a wonderful flavoring agent in cooking.

CRÈME DE VIOLETTE

This cordial is made the same way as crème de rose, but violet petals are used instead of rose petals. It has an intriguing aroma and a beautiful color.

CURAÇAO

This is made from a variety of bitter green orange, mace, cloves, and cinnamon, and sweetened with wine brandy.

DRAMBUIE

This is a liqueur made from Scotch whiskey and wild honey.

FALERNUM

This is a West Indian flavoring agent prepared from herbs, limes, and rum. It has a low alcoholic content, about 6 per cent, but it adds the most unusual flavor to gin and rum drinks. It is rather sweet.

FLOR ALPINA

This is a sweet Italian cordial which is put out in a tall bottle, usually with a stalk of the crystalline tree in the bottle which is heavily encrusted with sugar.

FRAISETTE

This cordial is made from alcoholic syrup, white wine, and strawberries.

FRAMBOISE
This cordial, which has a high alcoholic content, is made from raspberries.

GOLDWASSER
This cordial is also known as *Eau de Vie de Dantzig*, which is the French name, or *Danzig Goldwasser*, which is the German name. The French cordial is a distillation of fruit peels, herbs, and spices with an alcohol base. The German has a caraway seed flavor. Both have flecks of gold leaf added to them. Goldwasser is reputed to be the oldest cordial made, and strangely enough, was first made by the Italians.

GRAND MARNIER
In the opinion of a great many people, this is one of the finest cordials made. It is composed of white curaçao and *fine champagne* (the finest type of brandy).

KÜMMEL
This cordial, which is flavored with caraway and cumin seeds, is believed to have originated in Russia. It is very popular in Germany. As a matter of fact, *kümmel* is German for caraway seed.

MARASCHINO
This cordial, made from sour cherries and honey, is white and is used largely as a flavoring agent. It is not to be confused with the red syrup contained in bottles of maraschino cherries.

PARFAIT AMOUR
This is a highly perfumed and very sweet cordial made from citron, cinnamon, coriander, and brandy. In French the name means "perfect love." Perhaps that is why it is a great favorite with *les belles filles* of France.

PRUNELLE
As the name indicates, this cordial is prepared from small Burgundian prunes and fine brandy.

SLIVOVITZ

This cordial is tremendously popular in Europe and has had some vogue in the United States. It is made from plums which are fermented and distilled. It is one of the few high-proof cordials.

STREGA

This is probably the best known Italian cordial and is very delicious. It is made from orange peel, spices, and strong spirits. Although very sweet, it is a delightful accompaniment for coffee.

HORS
2. D'OEUVRES

It has long been my considered opinion that the serving of hors d'oeuvres (or canapés or appetizers) indelibly stamps a host or hostess as discriminating or inept. If I were to paraphrase the great French epicure, Brillat-Savarin, I'd say, "Show me what hors d'oeuvres you serve, and I'll tell you the caliber of your dinner."

It seems to me there are three approaches to the hors d'oeuvres question. Are you going to serve appetite whets with cocktails or other libations in the living room? Or are you going to serve hors d'oeuvres as a first course at dinner? Or are you serving appetizers and/or canapés at a cocktail party? The answer to any one of those three questions can well determine what sort of hors d'oeuvres are best to serve.

As appetite whets, hors d'oeuvres should be extremely simple, few in number, and should stimulate the appetite rather than satiate it. And they should not be served as blotters for a flock of hard liquor.

If they are served as a first course at the dinner table, they should again not be too heavy or filling, or of great amount. They should still put a hungry edge on appetite, and that can be accomplished by making them not only appealing to the taste, but also to the eye.

At a cocktail party, where dinner is not indicated, you can go to town as far as hors d'oeuvres are concerned. The only limit you need consider is your purse.

Here is a marvelous spread for unsalted crackers or silver-dollar-thin slices of icebox rye bread. But keep 'em few in number, for they'll go fast.

PÂTÉ OF CHICKEN LIVERS AND MADEIRA

½ lb. chicken livers	Thyme
1 large Bermuda onion	Salt
6 tbsp. chicken fat	Pepper
	Madeira

Slice a large Bermuda onion very thin and sauté it in 3 tablespoons of preheated chicken fat until it is golden brown. In another pan sauté for about 5 minutes ½ pound of chicken livers in 3 tablespoons of hot chicken fat, to which a pinch of thyme has been added, and salt and pepper to taste. Now mix the onion and the chicken livers together, and put them through a food grinder, using the finest blade. When the mixture has cooled, add enough Madeira to make a paste, spread on unsalted crackers or bread, and serve.

Pâté de foie gras, like caviar, is strictly a rich man's dish. It is superlatively good, but also superlatively expensive. A tiny earthenware crock containing hardly enough *pâté de foie gras* to put in your eye costs around $3.65 a copy!

I am very fond of *pâté de foie gras*, not only as an appetizer spread on unsalted crackers, but as a cooking ingredient. One of my pet dishes is Tournedos of Beef Rossini, which is broiled filet mignon placed on a slice of toast spread with *pâté de foie gras*, and a rich mushroom gravy poured over.

However, not having the income of a Las Vegas night club star, it is damn seldom that I serve the Tournedos. So I decided to experiment. And, to my delight, the experiment was a success. The result is what I call a "Poor Man's *Pâté de Foie Gras*," and I not only use it now in preparing Tournedos of Beef Rossini, but I serve it as an appetizer on unsalted crackers. All except those with a very discriminating palate will never know the difference, and (but don't let this get noised around) I've even fooled some gourmets!

POOR MAN'S PÂTÉ DE FOIE GRAS

½ lb. liverwurst sausage
1 3-oz. pkg. cream cheese
4 tbsp. mayonnaise
⅓ cup cream
1 tbsp. melted butter
½ tsp. curry powder

1 tbsp. Worcestershire sauce
1 tbsp. dry sherry wine
¼ tsp. each salt and pepper
Tiny pinch cayenne pepper

Tiny pinch grated nutmeg

With a fork mash and blend the sausage, cream cheese, mayonnaise, and cream. Then add the remaining ingredients, blending everything thoroughly (an Osterizer electric blender does the job perfectly). Let chill in the refrigerator before serving.

I might say, due to the difference in curry powders, that you should start with ¼ teaspoon of curry powder, and taste. If necessary, add a little more, pinch by pinch, until you have the right effect. The curry powder should not be discernible, as such.

At La Maison Wood, when we dine *en famille*, we always have two cocktails apiece an hour or so before dinner. With the cocktails we sometimes munch on a few nuts, sometimes on a little garlic cheese or anchovy cheese (these are packaged commercially, and are really excellent) spread on crackers, and sometimes on our own special canapés. They are the most taste-teasing, tantalizing, and terrific canapés I have ever tasted (I know I'm immodest, but please forgive me). But one needs real will power to keep from devouring several, and thereby spoiling one's dinner. Take my advice, and don't make more than three apiece.

CHUTNEY AND PEANUT BUTTER CANAPÉS

1 pkg. Philadelphia cream cheese
4 ounces Major Gray's chutney

½ lb. of peanut butter,
  chunky style
¼ tsp. Lowry's salt

¼ tsp. Worcestershire
  sauce
Dry red wine

Mix and blend the above ingredients together with a
tablespoon, cutting the larger pieces in the chutney into
smaller ones before adding. Use only enough dry red wine
to moisten the mixture so that it can be spread easily.
This paste is at its best when spread on Triscuits, although it can be spread on crackers, or silver-dollar-thin
slices of icebox rye bread. This spread can be kept in a
covered jar in the refrigerator, and will remain in perfect condition for weeks.

Some years ago, when I was living in Chicago, I be-
longed to a club-within-a-club at the South Shore Country Club. This inner club was called the Salty Dogs. On
dance nights, or special occasions, our group was wont
to gather in our own clubrooms for nightcaps and midnight snacks. The "court jester" of the crowd, Gordon
Glaescher, delighted in ordering a cannibal sandwich
(ground raw beef on a slice of bread, and topped with a
raw egg). When it was set before him, it always elicited
mild shrieks of horror from the Silly Cats (the feminine
auxiliary of the Salty Dogs). It was from the Cannibal
Sandwich that I developed my Tartare Canapés.

TARTARE CANAPÉS

2½ lbs. ground round steak
1 lime, juice of
4 tbsp. dry red wine
3 cloves garlic, minced
¾ tsp. Tabasco sauce
2 tsp. dry mustard
1 tsp. salt

2 tbsp. Worcestershire
  sauce
1 tsp. hickory smoked salt
1 tsp. curry powder
1 tsp. Escoffier Sauce
  Diable
Drained capers

Put, or have your butcher put, the raw, lean round
steak through the meat grinder twice. Then, in a large
bowl, add the remaining ingredients, except the capers.
Blend the mixture thoroughly, using the hand and fin-

gers to squeeze, and then turn out onto a large plate or platter, making a round mound. Refrigerate for a couple of hours before serving.

To serve, have a bowl of drained capers beside the platter of seasoned ground meat, and a basket of icebox rye bread, cut silver-dollar thin. The guests spread the beef on the bread, and sprinkle a few capers over the top.

How many will this serve? Possibly 20, but I have seen guests eat 5 or 6 apiece in rapid succession. My wife, who was one of the leading shudderers at Gordon Glaescher's cannibal sandwiches, now eats Tartare Canapés with great gusto, and loves 'em!

One appetizer that all of my guests have absolutely raved over every time we have served them is what I have called a Torpedo Onion Canapé. It is at its succulent best when torpedo onions are used, because they are so delicate and sweet. However, I have never come across torpedo onions outside of California, so if you can't get them, you can use slices of sweet Bermuda or Spanish onions instead.

TORPEDO ONION CANAPÉ

Small English muffins   *Slices of sweet onion*
Butter   *McLaren's Imperial sharp*
Lemon juice   *Cheddar cheese*
                        Paprika

I order from my bakery English muffins made the size of a silver dollar (in diameter, not thickness). I cut each one in half, and spread the halves with butter, and and sprinkle over a little lemon juice. Then I place a slice of torpedo onion, cut about ¼ inch thick, on each muffin half. If you can't get the torpedo onions, pare slices of sweet Bermuda or Spanish onions to fit the muffin halves. Then cover the onion slices with a layer of McLaren's Imperial sharp Cheddar cheese. Sprinkle a little paprika over the top, and place the prepared muffin halves on a cookie sheet under the broiler flame. Watch it, and when the cheese begins to bubble, serve immediately. Figure on serving only two halves to each guest, and when they beg for more, be firm!

One of the most celebrated appetizers, or hors d'oeuvres, which can be served with predinner libations (champagne preferred) or as a first course is *Quiche Lorraine*.

Samuel Chamberlain, in his wonderful volume, *Bouquet de France*, defines *Quiche Lorraine* as "at heart an honest and simple tart, not difficult to make and delicious when hot." He further describes it as "a hot, flaky crust filled with cream and bacon, and often fortified with eggs, onions or ham."

Here is the recipe for *Quiche Lorraine*.

QUICHE LORRAINE

Unbaked pie crust shell	*4 tbsp. minced onion*
White of 1 egg	*3-4 eggs*
½ lb. grated Gruyère	*1-2 cups rich milk, or*
cheese	*cream*
1 tbsp. flour	*Salt*
6 slices bacon	*Dash cayenne pepper*

Make your favorite rich pie crust shell (9 inches), and brush the entire surface with white of egg after the shell is in the pie tin. This prevents any sogginess in the crust.

Dredge the grated Gruyère (or imported Switzerland) cheese with the flour, mixing well. Fry the bacon slices in a skillet until nicely crisp. Drain them on paper toweling, and cut in small pieces.

In the bacon fat sauté the minced onion until limp, then distribute the onion and the bacon pieces over the bottom of the unbaked pie shell. Cover the onion and bacon pieces with the mixture of grated cheese and flour.

Beat 3 eggs with 1 cup of rich milk (or 4 eggs with 2 cups of rich milk for a deeper tart), salt to taste, and add the small pinch of cayenne pepper. Pour this custard over the cheese.

Bake in a 400-degree oven for 15 minutes, then reduce

the temperature to 325 degrees, and bake for 30 minutes
longer, or until a knife comes clean from the custard
This recipe will serve 6 generously, or 8 scantily.

A popular French dish is *Aubergines Caviare,* which is
simply eggplant caviar. I'm not at all sure how it got its
name, because I don't think it tastes like caviar, but I
do know it is a mighty fine first course appetizer. Perhaps
one might say that it's the poor man's caviar.

EGGPLANT CAVIAR

1 *large eggplant*	2 *fresh tomatoes*
1 *large onion*	½ *cup olive oil*
1 *green pepper*	*Salt*
1 *clove garlic*	*Pepper*

2 *tbsp. dry white wine*

Put a whole eggplant in a 400-degree oven and bake
until soft (about an hour).

While cooking the eggplant, peel and chop 1 large
onion, chop 1 green pepper, having removed the seeds
and white part, and peel and chop 2 tomatoes.

In a skillet put ½ cup of fine olive oil and 1 clove of
crushed garlic. When the oil is hot, put in the chopped
onion and green pepper and simmer them until they are
tender but not brown.

Now, cutting off the stem, peel the baked eggplant and
chop it finely. Mix this with the chopped tomatoes, and
add this mixture to the onions and green peppers in
the skillet, along with salt and freshly ground black pepper to taste, and 2 tablespoons of dry white wine. Mix
everything thoroughly, and continue to cook gently until
the mixture is fairly thick. Cool, then place in the refrigerator. Serve very well chilled, with pumpernickel, or silver-dollar-thin pieces of icebox rye bread.

The lovely Lillian Russell loved Lobster Crème, and
restaurateurs teased her with it wherever she went. To

aid in her reducing, it is said that "Diamond Jim" Brady bought her a gold-plated bicycle with mother-of-pearl handles and diamonds and rubies on the spokes! But apparently the exercise only increased her appetite for Lobster Crème.

LOBSTER CRÈME

½ lb lobster meat, shredded	½ tsp. salt
½ can condensed cream of mushroom soup	¼ tsp. cayenne pepper
	Bread crumbs
2 tbsp. dry sherry	1 tbsp. butter
1 tbsp. chopped pimiento	12 2-inch toast rounds

Combine the lobster meat, mushroom soup, sherry, pimiento, salt, and cayenne pepper in the top of a double boiler. Also combine the bread crumbs and the melted butter. Heat the lobster mixture until very hot. Then spread on the toast rounds, cover with the bread-crumb mixture, and place under the broiler until browned. This makes 12 canapés.

This dish is a wonderful thing to start off a summer meal.

MINTED FRUIT CUP

1 can pineapple chunks	Sugar
Peeled segments of grapefruit	Fresh lemon juice
	Maraschino cherries
Sprigs of fresh mint	Gin

Empty a can of pineapple chunks and juice into a bowl, and add an equal amount of peeled segments of fresh grapefruit and several finely chopped mint leaves. Dredge all this with sugar, after having added some fresh lemon juice. Cover the bowl and put it in the refrigerator for at least 12 hours.

Serve in individual compotes, pouring over the fruit in each compote an ounce of gin, arranging two or three mint leaves in the center of each compote, and topping the whole with a large maraschino cherry. You'll have fun listening to your guests trying to figure out the flavor while they spoon with delight.

3. SOUP

Throughout the world "dinner" and "soup" are synonymous terms to millions of people. Among numberless European peasants soup is the principal, if not the only, meal of the day.

However, in this land of abundance which is America, the serving of soup is governed by various considerations, such as the type of meal, the number of courses, the weather, and appetites.

Soup is said to prepare the stomach for the voluptuous activity to follow, and at the same time to stimulate the palate to a keener anticipatory pitch. So, for an elaborate, multicourse dinner, the curtain may well rise on a cup of cunningly contrived consommé or bisque. For those with hearty appetites, a cup of soup is an excellent prelude to a simple dinner. In either case the soup should be frosty cold in warm weather and steaming hot in cold weather.

There comes a time in every life, I think, when the nightly routine of an entree, potatoes, vegetable, salad, and dessert becomes vapid, no matter how varied the dinners may have been. Well, that's the time to serve a one-dish meal of a rich and hearty soup. It will put the zing back in your taste buds, and warm you to the very cockles of your heart, particularly when the frosty fingers of Ole Man Winter begin to reach for you.

On chill October nights, the riotous colors of autumn sunsets, and air redolent with smoke rising from burning leaves, bring back nostalgic memories of my grandmother's home in a small Michigan town. Coming in from a late-afternoon hike, the softly lighted living room, with a crackling log fire, was the most cheerful spot in the whole world, or at least so it seemed. And what rich, savory smells drifted in from the kitchen, particularly on the night of a soup dinner. After we were seated at the dining-room table, the maid would bring in the big willow-pattern tureen, and then large, piping hot soup bowls. Grandmother would remove the lid from the tureen and ladle the bowls brimming full. Emma would pass them without spilling a drop. With the soup came fresh, hot bread, or crisped corn bread, and a salad of chilled greens from which slivers of carrots, celery, and parsnips peeped out. Dessert usually was apple pie accompanied by generous wedges of Herkimer County cheese, and strong black coffee, with milk for me.

One of Grandmother's pet soups was black bean soup, and to my mind it is one of the most delicious soups ever devised, particularly if it is made with Marsala instead of sherry.

BLACK BEAN SOUP

1 cup black beans	1 bay leaf
1 qt. cold water	¼ cup chopped onions
2 tbsp. butter	4 grains mustard seed
¼ cup chopped celery leaves	1 tsp. salt
	Small clove garlic
1 medium-sized carrot, chopped	Ham bone
	Cayenne pepper
1 stalk celery, cut up	¾ cup scalded cream
2 whole cloves	4 tbsp. Marsala
6 peppercorns	Thin lemon slices

Sliced hard-boiled eggs

Soak the black beans overnight in cold water. Drain, then add the beans to 1 quart cold water in a soup kettle and bring to a boil. In the meantime, sauté in about 2 tablespoons of butter over a gentle flame ¼ cup of chopped celery leaves, 1 medium-sized carrot, chopped,

1 stalk of celery, cut up, and ¼ cup of chopped onion until they just begin to brown. Add these to the beans, as well as 2 whole cloves, 6 peppercorns gently bruised, 1 bay leaf, 4 grains of mustard seed, 1 teaspoon of salt, a small clove of garlic, and a ham bone. Now let the whole thing simmer until the beans are tender—about 3½ hours. Add a little more water if it cooks away too much, as it probably will. At the end of the cooking time, remove the ham bone and press the soup through a sieve. Now reheat to the boiling point, taste for seasoning (a touch of cayenne pepper adds a great deal) and stir in ¾ cup of scalded cream and 4 tablespoons of Marsala. In serving, place a thin slice of lemon and a slice of hard-cooked egg in each soup plate or bowl, and pour the hot soup over them.

There are many recipes for onion soup. Some gourmets advocate cooking the onions until they are a dark brown, or even crisp and black. Others contend that the onions should not even be lightly browned. I belong to the latter school. Some people like their onion soup made very plain. Others perfer the addition of claret, sherry, or white wine. And I know of one recipe that calls for a cup of champagne!

In the center of Les Halles, Paris' great market place, there is a quaint, wonderful workingmen's café called Au Père Tranquille. The hucksters (not advertising men, please!) ate and drank downstairs, but upstairs, where there was a funny little orchestra, you got what many claimed to be the best onion soup in Paris. Here's the recipe for that café's famous onion soup, which you can make right in your own home, whether it's *tranquille* or not.

ONION SOUP

12 to 16 red onions	2 tbsp. sugar
¼ cup olive oil	6 cups beef broth
4 tbsp. butter	4 tbsp. brandy
Salt	French bread
Pepper	Grated Parmesan cheese

Peel and thinly slice the red onions (red onions make for strength, and you want plenty), cutting them on the bias to avoid rings. Put ¼ cup of olive oil in a casserole, and add the sliced onions. Cook them very gently, and when they begin to tender, add 4 tablespoons of butter, salt and pepper to taste, and 2 tablespoons of sugar. When the onions have attained the limpid state, add 6 cups or so of rich beef broth, or canned beef bouillon, and let the whole simmer for 15 to 20 minutes. While the simmering is going on, toast slices of French bread. When the bread is toasted and buttered, sprinkle the slices with plenty of grated Parmesan cheese (fresh, not the packaged commercial kind, please!) and pop them under the broiler for a moment so they will be slightly browned. When you put the toast under the broiler, add 4 tablespoons of brandy to the soup, stirring it in gently. Then take out the toasted bread, fill each soup plate with the soup, float the toasted bread on top, and serve quickly. If you like more cheese, grate it and serve it separately. This recipe should serve six. Try it sometime for Sunday breakfast when the Saturday night libations have been *really* rugged.

Of all the so-called "peasant soups," I think the Italian minestrone is the most imposing, zestful and satisfying. Just the heavenly odors that emanate from the soup pot make my taste buds do nip-ups, and to wait for its completion would try the patience of Job himself.

The basis for minestrone is a bean broth, and there must be spicy meat in it along with lots of vegetables and *pasta*. I personally like my minestrone to be thick enough so that the spoon can stand upright in it.

MINESTRONE

½ cup kidney beans	Salt
¼ lb. bacon	Pepper
¼ lb. ham	Allspice
¼ lb. Italian sausage	2 quarts soup stock
2 cloves garlic	2 cups shredded cabbage
1 onion	1 cup Italian red wine

2 *stalks celery*   1 #2 *can tomatoes*
1 *zucchini (Italian squash)*   ½ *cup elbow macaroni*
1 *leek*   ¼ *cup fresh basil*
                Parmesan cheese

Soak ½ cup of kidney beans overnight in cold water (Roman beans are the best, if you can get them at an Italian grocery store; or lima beans can be used).

In a heavy skillet fry together until brown ¼ pound each of chopped bacon, chopped lean ham, chopped Italian sausage (*salsiccia*), and 2 crushed cloves of garlic. Then add 1 peeled and sliced onion, 2 stalks of celery, diced, 1 zucchini, sliced, 1 leek, sliced, salt and pepper to taste, and a pinch of allspice. Let simmer for 10 minutes.

In a soup kettle heat 2 quarts of consommé or soup stock. Put the contents of the skillet into the stock, and add the beans, which have been drained, 2 cups of shredded cabbage, and 1 cup of dry red wine. Simmer until the beans and vegetables are tender, about 1½ hours. Now add 1 #2 can of tomatoes (Italian if you can get it) and ½ cup of elbow macaroni. Cook about 15 minutes longer. About 3 minutes before the soup is to be served, add ¼ cup of finely minced basil (fresh if you have it, or 1 tbsp. dried). If the soup is too thick for your taste, it can be thinned out to your preference with more hot consommé. Grated Parmesan cheese should be passed in a bowl, and generously sprinkled on each plate.

Of course, there are some soups whose unusual flavor, or combination of flavors, just can't be retained in a can. One of these is mulligatawny. It is of East Indian origin, and the word means "pepper water." Consequently, the soup should be highly seasoned. In old England it was more commonly known as Curry Soup, and, indeed, the original recipe consisted of a rich, thin cream soup flavored with curry powder and plenty of spices, with small pieces of chicken cut up in it, and served with a dish of highly seasoned Indian rice. However, through the years it has changed somewhat, but, with the exception of the sherry, which I think adds a good deal to it, the following is what you might well expect to find in any of the outstanding restaurants or hotels in India.

MULLIGATAWNY SOUP

1 *large chicken*	2 *bay leaves*
¼ *cup butter*	½ *tsp. mace*
2 *medium-sized onions*	1 *tsp. allspice*
1 *clove garlic*	8 *peppercorns*
1 *stalk celery*	3 *cloves*
½ *green pepper*	½ *cup lentils*
1 *tart apple*	¼ *cup grated coconut*
1 *tbsp. flour*	*Coconut milk*
1 *tbsp. curry powder*	4 *cups chicken broth*
1 *tsp. salt*	¼ *cup sherry*
	Boiled rice

Cut up a good-sized chicken as for fricassee, roll in seasoned flour, and brown on all sides in ¼ cup of butter in a heavy pot. Add 2 medium-sized onions, minced, 1 clove of garlic, crushed, 1 stalk of celery, diced, ½ green pepper, minced, 1 tart apple, peeled, cored, and diced. Cook this mixture for about 5 minutes, then sprinkle in 1 tablespoon of flour, 1 tablespoon of curry powder mixed with 1 teaspoon of salt, 2 bay leaves, ½ teaspoon of mace, 1 teaspoon of allspice, 8 peppercorns, 3 cloves, ½ cup of lentils which have been soaked in cold water overnight, and ¼ cup of grated coconut which has been moistened with some of the coconut milk. (If you can't get fresh coconut, or you don't want to bother with it, use the packaged coconut that is grated. But the fresh coconut is more than worth the bother.) Next, add 4 cups of the chicken broth or bouillon. Simmer gently for at least 1 hour, or until the chicken is tender. Then remove the pieces of chicken from the pot, and strain the remainder of the pot into a large saucepan, pressing the vegetables, etc., through the sieve. Remove the meat from the chicken pieces, dice, and add it to the strained soup along with ¼ cup of dry sherry. Simmer once more, and serve very hot in plates or bowls in which 1 teaspoon of boiled rice has been placed.

While today it is possible to obtain excellent turkeys the year round, the Little Woman and I are rather old-fashioned about our national bird. We wait until Thanksgiving for our first turkey, and consequently we enjoy it to the utmost. The phrase, "My God, do we have cold turkey again tonight?" is never heard in La Maison Wood. And when the last meal is eaten from the succulent bird, we drool in anticipation of turkey soup.

TURKEY SOUP

Turkey carcass	3 tbsp. flour
Water	¼ cup uncooked rice
2 bay leaves	½ cup celery
Salt	Turkey meat
Pepper	Turkey gravy
Generous pinch marjoram	Turkey dressing
Generous pinch thyme	2 cups fresh mushrooms
Generous pinch basil	1 lb. chestnuts
Butter	3 tbsp. Madeira
Consommé	½ cup cooking oil

After having cut or torn away every particle of meat from your turkey carcass, break it up and put it in a large pot, along with 2 bay leaves, salt and pepper, and a generous pinch each of marjoram, thyme, and basil. Cover the carcass with water, and let it simmer slowly for 3 to 4 hours. Then remove the bones and strain the resulting broth through a sieve. This is your stock.

Melt 2 tablespoons of butter in a saucepan, and into it stir 3 tablespoons of flour until smooth. Gradually stir in the stock (which should amount to about 1½ to 2 quarts) and bring to a boil. Now add ¼ cup thoroughly washed uncooked rice, ½ cup of finely cut celery, additional salt and pepper to taste, and cook gently until the rice is soft—about 25 or 30 minutes.

In the meantime sauté in a couple of tablespoons of butter, 2 cups of fresh mushrooms, halving them if they are medium-sized, or quartering them if they are large, for about 5 minutes, and add them to the soup.

While the turkey stock has been simmering, prepare the chestnuts. Pick over enough chestnuts to have a pound of sound nuts. With a sharp, pointed knife cut the skin on the flat side of the chestnuts crisscross fashion. Then in a large skillet heat about ½ cup of cooking oil, add the chestnuts, and let them heat over a fast flame for about 4 or 5 minutes, shaking the pan and stirring the chestnuts all the while. Then drain them and let them stand until they are cool enough to handle (but not cold) and with a sharp knife remove the shell and skin. Put them in a saucepan, cover with canned consommé, and let them cook until they are tender. Then, when you have added the mushrooms to the soup, rub the chestnuts through a sieve and add them to the soup. Also add the diced turkey meat, any turkey gravy you have left over, and any dressing that remains.

Let all this simmer very, very gently until dinner time. Just before serving, add 3 tablespoons of Madeira, stirring it in.

As a rule I am not too fond of cooked cabbage. My mother and father loved a New England boiled dinner, but when I was served, I used to tell Dad to "skip the cabbage." However, I really go for the following combination of ham and cabbage, and I think you will too some frosty night.

HAM AND CABBAGE SOUP

2 tbsp. butter	2 cups cubed cooked ham
¼ cup chopped onion	1 bay leaf
¼ cup chopped celery	¼ tsp. salt
¼ cup chopped green pepper	⅛ tsp. pepper
3 cups boiling water	¾ cup sour cream
3 tbsp. flour	2 oz. Madeira wine
2 cups shredded cabbage	2 tbsp. chopped parsley

In a heavy pan lightly fry the onion, celery, and green pepper in the butter until the vegetables are clear. Re-

move from the heat and blend in the flour. Then slowly
add the boiling water, stirring constantly to blend well.
Return to the heat and add the cabbage, ham, bay leaf,
and salt and pepper to taste. Cook 8 to 10 minutes, or
until the cabbage is tender. Remove the bay leaf and
add the sour cream, mixing it in well. Let heat, and just
before serving stir in gently the Madeira wine. In serving,
sprinkle chopped parsley over each portion. This serves 4.

Of all the soups we have ever served in our home, the
one which never fails to draw extravagant praise is Crab
Bisque Helen. It is the creation of Helen Gruber, of
Carmel, California, wife of Brigadier General William
Gruber, USA, Retired.

CRAB BISQUE HELEN

12 oz. (1½ cups) crab meat	½ tsp. sugar
2 oz. butter	1 tsp. chili powder
½ small green pepper	2 tbsp. flour
1 medium onion	1 pint thin cream
4 tbsp. dry sherry	

Melt the butter in a saucepan, and in it sauté the green
pepper, seeded and finely minced, and the onion, also
minced, until they are transparent, but not browned.
While they are cooking, mix the sugar, chili powder, and
flour together in a bowl, blending the ingredients well
and making sure that any little lumps of chili powder
are smoothed out.

When the green pepper and onions are transparent,
add the flour-sugar-chili powder mixture slowly to the
saucepan, stirring constantly so that everything is well
blended. Then add the cream, continuing to stir all the
time. Let this simmer slowly until it has the consistency
of a cream sauce—about 10 minutes or so.

Put the crab meat in the top of a double boiler and
add the sherry to it. Let this heat through, then add the
crab meat and sherry to the sauce, mixing it in gently so

that the crab meat will not be broken up too much. Serve very hot.

For those who cannot obtain fresh crab meat, canned crab meat can be used. But the best substitute for fresh crab meat is fresh-frozen crab meat. My favorite is Wakefield's Ocean Frosted King Crab Meat. The Alaskan king crabs are caught, cleaned, cooked, and frozen at sea aboard trawlers. This frozen crab meat is ideal for any cooked crab meat dishes, or for cocktails and appetizers. Of course, it should be completely defrosted. I have found the best way to do this is to spread the frozen crab meat as it comes from the package out on towels, so that every bit of water will be absorbed.

Rum has always been a delightful flavoring agent for many kinds of desserts. Pies, puddings, and ice creams can rise to great gastronomic heights with the addition of rum to the recipe. However, rum as an ingredient in other dishes seems to be known only to a few, so I'm going to let you in on a few secrets here and there. The first is Shrimp Bisque with Rum.

SHRIMP BISQUE WITH RUM

1 *can condensed tomato soup*	1 *cup sweet cream*
1 *can condensed pea soup*	1 *lb. boiled shrimps*
	1½ *oz. light rum*

Stir the tomato and pea soup together, (after opening the cans, of course) until thoroughly mixed, in a saucepan or in the top of a double boiler. Then add 1 cup of sweet cream and blend it thoroughly with the soup mixture. Next, add 1 pound of fresh boiled shrimps (if they are jumbo shrimps, break them in half) and bring the whole thing to a boil, stirring slowly. When the mixture comes to a boil, add 1½ ounces of light rum, stir it in well, remove from the fire, and serve.

Cioppino is something like *bouillabaisse*, yet to my mind it is more lusty and flavorsome than any bouillabaisse one can get in America. *Cioppino* usually consists of various shellfish and pieces of fish, put in a pot, then covered with a rich garlic sauce, and cooked for 15 to 20 minutes. The first *Cioppino* I ate had the shellfish left in their shells (which makes it more toothsome, to my mind). But it can be made with the shellfish removed from their shells.

The following recipe, which I devised, is sort of a composite of different recipes from Fisherman's Wharf restaurants in San Francisco.

CIOPPINO

¼ cup olive oil
8 oz. butter
2 medium onions, chopped
1 leek, diced
2 green peppers, diced
4 cloves garlic, minced
2 #2 cans solid pack
    tomatoes
1 6-oz. can tomato paste
2 cups canned tomato sauce
1 bay leaf
2 pinches dried oregano

2 pinches dried thyme
2 pinches dried basil
6 whole peppercorns
1 pinch cayenne pepper
Salt and pepper
1¾ cups dry white wine
¼ cup Marsala wine
2 medium lobsters
4 hard-shell crabs
1 lb. raw shrimps
12 oysters
24 clams

2 lbs. firm-fleshed fish

In a large skillet heat the olive oil (use only the best, which to my mind is Old Monk) and butter, then add the onions, chopped, the leek, diced, the green peppers, seeded and diced, and the garlic, minced. Sauté these until lightly browned, then add the tomatoes, tomato paste, canned tomato sauce, bay leaves, dried oregano, dried thyme and basil, the peppercorns, slightly bruised, cayenne pepper, and salt and pepper to taste. Cover, and cook the sauce very, very slowly over the lowest possible flame, stirring frequently, for 2 hours. Then add the dry white wine and the Marsala wine, and cook for 10 minutes more.

In the meantime cook the lobsters, crabs, and shrimps (these last should be shelled and deveined) in boiling

salted water until tender, 10 to 15 minutes. Allow the
oysters and clams, covered with fresh water, to stand
for 1 hour, then scrub the shells thoroughly. Have 2
pounds of flaky fish, such as sea bass, rock cod, red snap-
per, or other firm-fleshed fish, cleaned, boned, and cut in
2-inch pieces.

Place the seafood in layers in a deep pot or kettle
(split the lobsters in half and crack the claws), pour the
sauce over all, cover the pot, and simmer on top of the
stove for 15 to 20 minutes. Serve in deep soup plates,
and accompany with hot garlic bread, and chilled dry
white wine. This recipe may serve 8, depending upon
appetites.

I suppose *Vichyssoise* is the swankiest of all soups.
I've never seen *Vichyssoise* on the menus of Main Street
lunchrooms, or, for that matter, on the menus of ordinary, good, run-of-the-mill eating places. But it's seldom,
if ever, omitted from the *cartes des jours* of the top
restaurants and hotels. But the notion that it is difficult
to make at home is definitely old hat. If you don't believe
me, try this out for kicks and a real taste thrill.

VICHYSSOISE

4 *leeks*	2 *tbsp. chopped parsley*
1 *medium-sized onion*	5 *medium-sized potatoes*
1 *medium-sized carrot*	3 *cups medium cream*
½ *cup butter*	*Salt*
2 *stalks celery*	*Pepper*
5 *cups chicken broth*	*Cayenne pepper*
1 *cup medium dry white*	⅛ *tsp. mace*
wine	1 *cup heavy cream*
	Minced chives

Thinly slice 4 leeks (white part only) and sauté in ½
cup of butter, together with 1 medium-sized onion, thinly
sliced, 1 medium-sized carrot, thinly sliced, and 2 stalks
of celery, chopped, until lightly browned—about 10
minutes—in a pot. Then add 5 cups of chicken broth and
1 cup of medium dry California white wine to the pot,

along with 2 tablespoons of chopped parsley and 5 medium-sized peeled potatoes, sliced thin. Boil for 30 minutes or so.

Strain the mixture into a saucepan, forcing the solids through a sieve. Add 3 cups of medium cream. Season with salt and white pepper to taste, add a pinch of cayenne pepper and ⅛ teaspoon of mace, and bring to a boil. Remove from the fire and allow to cool, then place in the refrigerator and chill thoroughly.

Before serving, add 1 cup of chilled heavy cream, whip with a rotary beater for 1 or 2 minutes, and serve, topping each serving with minced chives.

CAUTION: To prevent discoloration, cool the strained soup in enamel, china, or stainless steel utensil.

4. FISH

Erasmus, the great Dutch theologian of the Renaissance, despised fish. "My heart," he said, "is Catholic, but my stomach is Lutheran." Perhaps he lived in boardinghouses (if such things existed during the fifteenth and sixteenth centuries) and couldn't face Fridays, with the lukewarm, greasy, and hard-crusted hunks of fish on the table.

The French are probably the greatest fish cooks in the world. Certainly no other cuisine has as many delectable methods of preparing and cooking fish. Dione Lucas, in her excellent *Cordon Bleu Cook Book* devotes 90 pages to fish recipes, with 45 recipes for fillet of sole alone.

The deliciousness of many of the French recipes for fish is due to the use of herbs and wine. Thyme, tarragon, parsley, and bay leaf (but used sparingly) lend their piquancy to fish, and for nearly all the great fish dishes wine is a necessity. In fact, in no other phase of cooking is wine so important, because it points up so beautifully the delicate flavor of the fish.

The chances are that when you go into any but the high-priced and exclusive eating places and order fillet of sole, you will get flounder. Actually, the flounder is a family name that includes gray sole and lemon sole. The true English sole, however, is very scarce in this country; but with overseas air express it is becoming available in American markets. If you can get the English sole, use them in the recipes which follow. If not, you can't go too wrong with fillets of flounder.

FILLET OF SOLE AU VIN BLANC

4 *large or 8 small fillets of*	1 *bay leaf*
sole	1 *cup dry white wine*
1 *tbsp. butter*	½ *cup consommé*
1 *tsp. chopped onion*	*Salt*
1 *tsp chopped parsley*	*Pepper*
3 *mushrooms, chopped fine*	2 *tbsp. cream*
1 *stalk celery*	*Grated Parmesan cheese*

Salt and pepper 4 large or 8 small fillets of sole or flounder. In a large skillet melt 1 tablespoon butter and add 1 teaspoon chopped onion, 1 teaspoon chopped parsley, 3 mushrooms, chopped fine, 1 stalk of celery, chopped, 1 bay leaf, 1 cup California sauterne or Chablis, ½ cup consommé.

Lay fillets in the hot liquid and let simmer 5 to 10 minutes, until barely tender. Remove carefully to shallow baking dish. Boil down the liquid in which fish was cooked until about ¾ cup remains. Add 2 tablespoons cream, and more seasonings if needed. Strain the liquid over fish in baking dish, sprinkle grated Parmesan cheese over all, and bake on upper shelf of hot oven (450 degrees) for about 10 minutes, or until top is lightly browned. (Serves 4.)

This recipe is prepared with fresh tomatoes—and I do mean fresh tomatoes.

FILLET OF SOLE WITH FRESH TOMATOES

4 *fillets of sole*	1 *cup dry white wine*
Salt	½ *cup cream*
Pepper	4 *tomatoes*
3 *tbsp. butter*	1 *tsp. chopped parsley*
1 *medium-sized onion*	*Pinch tarragon*
2 *little green onions*	*Pinch thyme*

1 *clove garlic*   *Pinch basil*
1½ *tbsp. flour*   ¼ *cup fine bread crumbs*
   2 *tbsp. grated Parmesan cheese*

Place 4 fillets of sole in a well-buttered baking dish, and season to taste with salt and freshly ground pepper.

Melt 3 tablespoons of butter in a saucepan. Add 1 medium-sized onion, peeled and chopped, 2 little green onions, chopped, and 1 clove of garlic, minced, and sauté for about 5 minutes without browning. Then stir in 1½ tablespoons of flour, and add 1 cup of dry American white wine. Bring to a boil, then slowly add ½ cup of cream. Simmer for about 5 minutes, season with salt and pepper to taste, add 4 tomatoes, peeled, seeded, and coarsely chopped, and finally 1 teaspoon chopped parsley and a pinch each of dried tarragon, thyme, and basil.

Pour this sauce over the sole. Sprinkle over all about ¼ cup of fine bread crumbs and a couple of tablespoons of grated Parmesan cheese. Put in a moderate oven (350 degrees) for about 15 to 20 minutes. Remove and serve.

A perfect sauce for fillet of sole is Sauce Marguery. The essence of this sauce is the concentrated fish stock artfully flavored with herbs, and combined with wine. It originated in the famous old Café Marguery in Paris. Sauce Marguery is relatively inexpensive. Its exquisite flavor is due to an artful blending of herbs, all of which are on the shelves of practically all groceries. So, why don't you try this wonderful dish?

FILLET OF SOLE MARGUERY

10 *small fillets of sole* 6 *cups water*
¼ *cup carrots, sliced* ½ *tsp. salt*
2 *leeks, sliced*   ⅛ *tsp. pepper*
1 *tbsp. parsley flakes* 8 *mussels (or oysters)*
10 *peppercorns, bruised* 8 *small shrimps, boiled*
1 *bay leaf*   4 *oz. dry white wine*
⅛ *tsp. dried thyme*   ¼ *lb. butter*
     4 *egg yolks*

Place 2 of the fillets of sole in a large pot. Add the carrots, leeks, parsley, peppercorns, bay leaf, dried thyme, and water. Bring to a boil, then simmer until the liquid is reduced by half, then remove from the fire and strain, reserving the broth and discarding the solids. This is your fish stock.

Place the remaining 8 fillets of sole in a baking dish and cover with 1 cup of the reserved fish stock. Place in a 375-degree oven and simmer for 10 to 15 minutes, or until fish is tender. Drain off the stock, and simmer it again in a saucepan until it is reduced to about 4 tablespoons. Gently fold each fillet in half and sprinkle with salt and pepper. Top each fillet with 1 shrimp and 1 mussel (or oyster).

Place the 4 tablespoons of reduced fish stock in the top of a double boiler. Add 3 ounces of the dry white wine, then the butter, and cook over very gently boiling water in the bottom of the double boiler until butter is melted. Beat the egg yolks until lemon-colored, then add to them the remaining 1 ounce of wine. Add this egg yolk-wine mixture to the butter-stock-wine mixture, stirring constantly, and cook until it is the consistency of a medium cream sauce. Strain this sauce over the fillets, and place under a medium broiler flame until lightly browned. Serves 4 to 6.

As a rule I don't care much for boiled fish, but I think salmon lends itself particularly to boiling, and, with a shrimp or lobster sauce, it is really a gourmet dish. Here's a recipe for Boiled Salmon with Shrimp Sauce, but if you wish, you can substitute lobster for the shrimp.

BOILED SALMON WITH SHRIMP SAUCE

2 lb. salmon	Salt
2 qt. white wine	Pepper
1 tbsp. butter	1 egg yolk
1 tbsp. flour	1 cup cream
½ lb. cooked shrimps	2 tbsp. Madeira

Bring the wine to the boiling point.

Wrap about 2 pounds of salmon in cheesecloth, and lower it into the boiling wine. Cover, and simmer for about 20 to 30 minutes, then remove the pot from the fire.

In the top of a double boiler melt 1 tablespoon of butter. Blend in 1 tablespoon of flour. Add ½ pound of cooked shrimps, cut in pieces, and ½ cup of the wine the salmon has been boiled in, and salt and pepper to taste. Let cook for 3 minutes. Beat 1 egg yolk and pour over it a cup of scalded cream, then add this to the broth and shrimps.

Place the salmon on a hot platter. Add 2 tablespoons of Madeira to the shrimp sauce, blend, and pour over salmon.

The flesh of the salmon is rich and delicious in flavor, and may be cooked in almost any manner. It is equally savory when served cold. And, as an added feature, salmon always has terrific eye appeal.

I have experimented until I have come up with what I consider the most delicious broiled fresh salmon I have ever tasted. And it is very easy to prepare and cook.

BROILED FRESH SALMON

2 *medium-sized fresh salmon*   Salt
    steaks, 1 inch thick   *Freshly ground pepper*
Lime juice   *4 pinches dried tarragon*
Butter   *leaves*
          4 oz. dry vermouth

Place the salmon steaks in a shallow, fireproof baking pan and squeeze lime juice over them. Then dot them liberally with butter, sprinkle with salt and freshly ground pepper, and a pinch (for each steak) of dried tarragon leaves. Pour about 4 ounces of dry (French) vermouth in the pan around the steaks, but not over them.

Place the pan under the broiler, about 4 inches from the flame. Cook for about 10 to 12 minutes, basting carefully once or twice during the latter part of the cooking, so that the herbs will not be "washed off" the surface of the steaks. Then turn the steaks, season as before, and broil for about 5 to 6 minutes, again basting with the vermouth after the seasonings have been "set" by the heat. If necessary, add a little more vermouth to the pan.

The steaks will be moist, tender, and have the most intriguing flavor you have ever tasted. With this, serve parsley potatoes, a good coleslaw, and a chilled dry white wine.

Pompano en Papillotte (pompano cooked in paper cases) is probably one of the swankiest and most delectable dishes in the realm of fish cookery. In the first place pompano, with its rich, delicately flavored flesh, is considered to be one of the choicest of salt-water fishes. And the cooking of it in a sealed paper bag, laved with an ambrosial sauce made with shellfish and wine, only enhances its deliciousness.

Antoine's Restaurant, in the old French Quarter of New Orleans, is one of the finest restaurants in the world. Its age (over a hundred years), its picturesqueness, and its high culinary tradition carried on by three generations of the Alciatore family, make it unique. And it was in this restaurant that *Pompano en Papillotte* was originated.

The following recipe is the original one as devised by Jules Alciatore. It was given to me by my dear friend Roy Alciatore, Jules' son, with special permission for its use in this book. Its preparation is tricky work, but Roy gives the assurance that anyone can turn out this specialty.

POMPANO EN PAPILLOTTE ANTOINE'S

3 *medium-sized pompano*	6 *tbsp. butter*
3 *cups water*	½ *clove garlic, minced*
1 *chopped shallot (or 2 tbsp.*	1 *cup diced cooked shrimps*
chopped onion)	8 *chopped onions (1½ cups)*
2 *tbsp. flour*	*Pinch dried thyme*
2 *egg yolks*	1 *bay leaf*

2¼ cups dry white wine   2 cups fish stock
1 cup crab meat   Salt and pepper

Clean the pompano, and cut them into 6 fillets, removing head and backbone (your fish dealer can fillet the pompano for you, but be sure you get the head and bones, as this is the basis for the fish stock). Combine the head and bones and water, and simmer until there are 2 cups of stock remaining. Sauté the shallot (or the 2 tablespoons of chopped onion) and the fillets of pompano in 2 tablespoons of butter for a couple of minutes, then add 2 cups of dry white wine, cover, and simmer the whole gently until the fillets are tender, about 5 to 8 minutes.

In another saucepan sauté the crab meat and shrimps and ¼ clove of garlic, minced, in 1 tablespoon of butter for a minute or so, then add the other ¼ clove of garlic and the 1½ cups of chopped onion, and cook for 10 minutes. Add the thyme, bay leaf, and 1¾ cups of fish stock, and simmer for another 10 minutes. Blend together 2 tablespoons each of butter and flour, and gradually add the remaining ¼ cup of fish stock. Add this to the crab meat-shrimp mixture along with the wine stock drained from the fillets. Cook, stirring constantly, until thickened. Beat the egg yolks, and add the hot sauce and the remaining ¼ cup of dry white wine. Mix thoroughly, and place in the refrigerator until firm.

Cut 6 parchment paper hearts 8 inches long and 12 inches wide. Oil well, and lay a poached fillet on 1 side of the heart, and cover the fillet with spoonfuls of sauce. Fold the heart over, and hand-seal the edges. Lay the sealed hearts on an oiled baking sheet, and bake in a 450-degree oven for 15 minutes, or until the paper hearts are browned. Serve immediately in the paper hearts. This recipe serves 6.

Fillets of fresh salmon, sea bass, striped bass, sole, or flounder may be used instead of pompano.

The halibut might be mistaken for a gigantic overgrown flounder. It's a cold water fish, firm fleshed yet some-

what fat. Along with the cod and haddock, the halibut
supports many a family of New England fishermen.

While the halibut may be pan fried, sautéd or broiled,
I think it reaches its height of deliciousness in the following recipe.

BAKED CURRIED HALIBUT

2 lb. halibut steaks	1 small onion
1 cup dry white wine	½ green pepper
1 cup fine bread crumbs	1 stalk celery
Salt	3 tbsp. flour
Pepper	1 tsp. curry powder
6 oz. butter	Dash Tabasco
	1 tsp. lemon juice

Place 1 cup of dry California white wine in a dish, or
bowl, and dip the halibut steaks in the wine; then dip in
fine bread crumbs and sprinkle with salt and pepper.

Heat ¼ cup of butter in a fireproof baking dish in a
hot oven, 500 degrees. Place the bread-crumbed halibut
in the baking dish, baste with the hot butter, and bake uncovered for about 10 minutes, or until the crumbs are
browned and the fish begins to flake with a fork.

In a saucepan melt 2 ounces of butter and add 1 small
onion, peeled and minced, ½ green pepper, minced, and
1 stalk of celery, chopped. Sauté over a low flame for
10 minutes.

Blend 3 tablespoons of flour mixed with 1 teaspoon of
curry powder into the mixture, stirring constantly, and
add the remaining dry white wine. Stir well, add a dash of
Tabasco and 1 teaspoon of lemon juice. Bring to a boil,
stirring.

Arrange the halibut on a platter, and pour the hot
sauce over it.

A great many people think that the cod is strictly a
New England institution. Actually, continental Europe
holds the cod in high esteem, and *brandade de morue* is
one of the most popular dishes throughout France, where
it is often referred to as "the glory of Nîmes," the

town which it is said the dish hails from. If you have scorned creamed codfish, let me urge you to try the following method of preparing it, and two gets you six that you'll love it also.

BRANDADE DE MORUE
(Creamed Codfish)

1 *lb. salt codfish*	5 *tbsp. olive oil*
Garlic	1 *tbsp. minced parsley*
1 *tbsp. very dry white wine*	¼ *tsp. white pepper*
5 *tbsp. heavy cream*	*Pinch nutmeg*
	Pinch cayenne pepper

Soak 1 pound of salt codfish in cold water for 8 to 10 hours, changing the water twice. Drain, add enough cold water to cover the fish, and bring to the boiling point. Skim the water and set the fish aside to cool in the covered saucepan.

When the fish is cool, remove all bones and skin, and shred the fish very fine. (If you have a mortar and pestle, pound the shredded fish to a smooth paste. You can accomplish practically the same thing by putting the shredded fish in a crockery bowl, and using a heavy spoon or a cocktail muddler.) This is one of the secrets of a perfect *brandade de morue*.

Rub a split clove of garlic once around the top of a double boiler. You want just a hint of garlic flavor. Put the paste of codfish in the top of the double boiler and keep it hot on the fire. Now beat into it with a wooden spoon 1 tablespoon of very dry California white wine. Next add 3 ounces of slightly warmed olive oil very, very slowly (as in making mayonnaise), stirring constantly until it is perfectly blended. In the same manner add 3 ounces of warmed heavy cream. Then stir into the mixture a tablespoon of finely minced parsley, a small pinch each of cayenne pepper and nutmeg, and ¼ teaspoon of white pepper. Serve hot over triangles of not-too-thick toast. Baked potatoes are an ideal accompaniment, and a glass of chilled American Chablis or Riesling is indicated for additional pleasure.

Swordfish steaks are pretty terrific just plain broiled—
with a thin veil of flour over them and sautéed in plenty
of butter to keep the delicate meat from drying out.

It was on the Cape that a native Cape Codder told me
about a recipe for swordfish in white wine that she said
had come down from her forebears. Here is the recipe that
I finally wangled from her.

SWORDFISH IN WHITE WINE

1½ lb. swordfish	Salt
2 cups dry white wine	Pepper
½ cup water	6 bulbs little green onions
1 tbsp. chopped parsley	¼ lb. fresh mushrooms
1 tsp. chopped chives	1 tbsp. flour
1 stalk celery	2 egg yolks
Butter	½ cup cream

6 clams, chopped

Put 1½ pounds of swordfish in a deep skillet and pour
over it 2 cups of dry California white wine diluted with a
half cup of water. Add a tablespoon of chopped parsley,
a teaspoon of chopped chives, a single stalk of celery,
chopped, a tablespoon of butter, and salt and pepper to
taste, and let the whole thing simmer until the fish is done.

While the fish is simmering, fry 6 bulbs of little green
onions and ¼ pound of fresh mushrooms in butter. Sift
into this a tablespoon of flour. When this *roux* is well
blended, add it to the wine in which the fish has
boiled (after the fish is done, of course). Let this cook
a minute or two, and then thicken with the yolks of 2
eggs, beaten up with ½ cup of cream. Let this heat and
then add the clams to the sauce. When it is thoroughly
hot, pour the sauce over the fish, which has been ar-
ranged on a platter.

Here is an unusual recipe for noodles and tuna fish
which depends upon the blend of tropical spices in
Angostura bitters for a rare taste tang.

EPICURE'S DELIGHT

2 cups (about 4 oz.) noodles	2 tbsp. butter
2 tbsp. minced green pepper	1½ tbsp. flour
1 3-oz. can button mushrooms, drained	¾ tsp. salt
	1 cup milk
⅔ cup grated Cheddar cheese	1 tsp. Angostura bitters
¾ cup drained canned asparagus tips	Small pinch paprika
	¾ cup flaked tuna fish

Parsley

Cook the noodles in salted boiling water. When tender (about 12-14 minutes) drain through a collander. Then pour cold water over the noodles and drain again.

Melt the butter in the saucepan. Add the flour and blend well. Add ½ teaspoon of salt and add the milk gradually. Cook until it just begins to bubble. Add the noodles, asparagus tips, tuna fish, green pepper, paprika, ¼ teaspoon of salt, and the mushrooms. Add the Angostura bitters last, and mix everything gently but well. Put in a buttered casserole dish and sprinkle the grated cheese over the top (incidentally, I prefer grated Parmesan cheese). Bake in a 350-degree oven for 40 minutes. Serve hot, garnished with parsley. This recipe serves 6.

If you desire to use fresh mushrooms and asparagus tips, clean the asparagus and cook until tender, and use only the very tender top part. In using fresh mushrooms, wash and sauté them about 5 minutes in the 2 tablespoons of butter before making the white sauce.

5. SHELLFISH

From the vast stretches of sand worked over by the seas of the world come some of the greatest gastronomic delights known to man—shellfish.

The term "shellfish" embraces both mollusks and crustacea. Among the mollusks there are those with a single shell (the abalone), and those with two shells which open and close (clams, mussels, oysters, and scallops). Crustacea have a relatively thin segmented shell covering their bodies, that can usually be peeled off. Among this group of shellfish are crabs, crayfish, lobsters, prawns, and shrimp.

Shellfish must always be alive when purchased, unless they are frozen or already cooked. Among the bivalves a tightly closed shell indicates they are alive. Gaping shells that do not close when handled is proof that they are dead, and should not be used. Crabs and lobsters have a lively movement of their claws when alive, and they should remain alive up to the moment of cooking. Fresh prawns and shrimps, however, are generally marketed headless. They should be greenish in color and firm to the touch. Scallops are marketed already shucked. When absolutely fresh they will have a firm, white appearance.

One further warning. When buying cooked, whole lobsters, uncurl the tail. If it springs back when released, the lobster was alive when cooking started. If it doesn't, it was dead when cooked, and shun it!

CRABS

There are over one thousand varieties of crabs, and they are found all over the world. The best known varieties are the blue crab, from the Eastern seaboard and Gulf states; the rock crab from New England; the morro, or stone crab, from the South Atlantic coast; the large dungeness crab, weighing anywhere from 1½ to 3½ pounds, from the Northern Pacific coast; and the giant Alaskan king crab, weighing anywhere from 5 to 12 pounds, and measuring as much as 10 feet from claw to claw (I'd hate to meet one on a dark and stormy night!).

This latter crab has eight enormous uniform-sized claws, and little or no body meat. Two or three 10-inch segments usually constitute a serving, and are at their best when broiled. The meat is flecked with red. For the last decade frozen Alaskan king crab meat has been available. The crabs are caught, cleaned, cooked, and frozen aboard specially built trawlers operating off the Alaskan coast.

The late Ernest Byfield, of Chicago, gourmet extraordinary and restaurateur supreme, was not a gentleman chef. But he could, and did, invent some superb dishes.

At luncheon one day he told me about one of his creations, Crab Meat Louise. It seems that some years ago Grace Moore asked him to produce a dinner menu for a special party that she was going to give in the Pump Room of the Ambassador East Hotel, which was owned by the Byfields. So Ernie "dreamed up" the principal dish.

"Miss Moore's cosmopolitan palate," he said, "approved the dish very highly, and we added it to our Pump Room menu. It is terrific in flavor, and," he added with a grin, "terrific in calories."

Crab Meat Louise à la Byfield is indeed a terrific shellfish preparation. So, sometime when you want to splurge, toss your calorie counter in the fireplace and try a truly ambrosial dish.

There are three parts to the dish—Crab Meat Maryland, French pancakes, and a Sauce Mousseline.

CRAB MEAT LOUISE À LA BYFIELD
Crab Meat Maryland

3 *tbsp. butter*	1 *lb. fresh crab meat*
2 *tbsp. flour*	*Salt to taste*
1 *cup cream*	*Freshly ground pepper to taste*
1 *tbsp. chopped chives*	¼ *cup dry sherry wine*
Lemon juice	

French Pancakes

3 *eggs*	*Few grains salt*
2 *tbsp. twice-sifted flour*	1 *tbsp. cold water*
½ *tsp. butter (per cake)*	

Sauce Mousseline

4 *egg yolks*	2 *drops cold water*
½ *lemon (juice of)*	4 *oz. butter*
Brandy or cognac	

First, make the Crab Meat Maryland. Melt the butter in the top of a double boiler, the lower section half-filled with boiling water. Blend the flour with the cream until smooth, and add to the melted butter. Stir constantly until the mixture begins to thicken (about 5 minutes), then add the chopped chives and cook 5 minutes more, stirring constantly. Now add the picked-over fresh crab meat (or fresh-frozen crab meat that has been defrosted and dried), stir well but gently to avoid breaking up the meat, and heat through for 5 minutes. Season to taste with salt and freshly ground pepper, then add the sherry wine and a few drops of lemon juice. Turn the heat well down and keep the crab-meat mixture hot over the hot water in the bottom of the double boiler.

Next, make your French pancakes. In a mixing bowl place the eggs, the twice-sifted flour, the cold water, and a few grains of salt. Beat the mixture vigorously until it has the consistency of thin cream. In a small frying pan (5 inches in diameter) place ½ teaspoon of butter, and when it begins to bubble pour in about 1 generous tablespoon of batter, or just enough to cover the bottom of the pan. Shake the pan so as to distribute the batter evenly, and cook over a medium flame for 1 minute, then turn the pancake and cook another minute. Stack the cakes on top of each other until all are baked, and keep warm.

The third step is the Sauce Mousseline, which is essentially equal quantities of Hollandaise sauce and stiffly whipped cream stirred very carefully and constantly until the sauce is thoroughly heated, and seasoned to taste with salt and white pepper. Or it can be made by putting the yolks of 4 eggs in a small earthenware bowl, adding the juice of half a small lemon, a couple of drops of cold water, and 4 ounces of butter cut into small pieces. Stand the bowl in a saucepan full of boiling water and stir quickly with a wooden spoon; in a minute or two the sauce will be like soft cream, as it should be.

To complete the Crab Meat Louise, distribute the Crab Meat Maryland on the pancakes and roll them up. Then cover the rolled pancakes with the Sauce Mousseline. In serving, ladle burning cognac or brandy over each serving.

Crab Meat à la Charlotte is about the most delicious gourmet "quickie" I have ever tasted. It is the creation of Charlotte Morrissey, of San Francisco.

CRAB MEAT À LA CHARLOTTE

¾ lb. cooked crab meat	1 can cream chicken soup
1 can chicken gumbo soup	¼ tsp. Worcestershire
½ cup half & half (milk	sauce
& cream)	½ tsp. fine curry powder
	2 oz. dry sherry

In top of a double boiler put ¾ pound cooked crab meat, including legs, 2 cans condensed chicken gumbo soup, undiluted, ½ cup half & half, 2 ounces dry sherry, ½ teaspoon best curry powder, and ¼ teaspoon Worcestershire sauce. Mix all very gently, and cook over lightly boiling water until thoroughly heated through. Serve in soup plates or bowls, accompanied by crusty French bread and a tossed green salad. This serves 3 generously.

Ernie Byfield was famous for his Crab Meat in a Skillet, and I suspect that the Baked Imperial Crab Meat that is served in the Well of the Sea Restaurant of the Hotel Sherman in Chicago is a concoction that he devised. Anyway, it is a very piquant and delicious dish.

BAKED IMPERIAL CRAB MEAT

1 lb. fresh or frozen crab meat	1 cup white bread crumbs
	1 tsp. salt
¼ cup butter	6 drops Tabasco sauce
4 shallots (or ¼ onion)	½ lemon, juice of
2 tsp. A-1 sauce	2 tsp. dry white wine
1 tsp. Worcestershire sauce	1 egg
1 tsp. dry mustard	

Break the crab meat into large pieces. Chop shallots or onion finely and sauté in about 1 tablespoon of butter until transparent. Combine the remaining ingredients, reserving about ½ the bread crumbs, and mix well. Add the crab meat. Melt the remaining butter in skillet and add the crab-meat mixture. Cook until the bread crumbs are slightly browned.

Fill 4 scallop shells or shallow baking dishes with mixture, and top with buttered bread crumbs, using reserved bread crumbs and added butter. Bake in a 350-degree oven for about 30 minutes. This serves 4 portions.

The most epicurean of the crab family are the soft-shell crabs. These crabs are not a species; rather, the term is applied to any crab which has shed its old shell and whose new shell has not yet hardened. To my mind, it is a crime to dip this tender crustacean into a batter and fry it. They should always be sautéed in butter and served with lemon juice over them. However, when they are gently sautéed in butter and covered with a cham-

pagne and almond sauce, they are out of this world—
and the next.

SOFT-SHELL CRABS AMANDINE
WITH CHAMPAGNE SAUCE

12 *soft-shell crabs*	1 *tbsp. chopped chives*
Flour	1 *tbsp. chopped chervil, or*
Salt	*parsley*
Pepper	2 *cups champagne*
½ *cup blanched almonds*	3 *egg yolks*
6 *oz. butter*	½ *cup cream*
Cayenne pepper	

Get 12 soft-shell crabs and have your butcher prepare them for the stove for you, first telling him you are
going to sauté them. When you get them home, wash
them in cold water, then pat dry with paper toweling and
toss very lightly in seasoned flour.

Blanch and shred ½ cup of almonds, and sauté them
in about 2 tablespoons of hot butter until they are lightly browned.

In a heavy iron skillet melt 4 ounces of butter, and
when it is pubbling hot put in the crabs, shell side down.
Reduce the heat and sauté the crabs until browned.
After about 5 minutes, turn the crabs, and brown the
underside. Watch carefully during the browning process
that the crabs don't stick to the pan or burn. When the
crabs are nicely browned, remove from the skillet onto
a hot platter and keep warm.

To the butter in the skillet add 1 tablespoon of finely
chopped chives and a tablespoon of chopped chervil or
parsley. Then add 2 cups of American champagne and
simmer for about 5 minutes. Have ready the yolks of 3
eggs beaten together with ½ cup of cream. Add this to
the wine broth, being careful not to let the broth boil
after the egg mixture is added. Add a pinch of cayenne
pepper, salt to taste, and when the broth is thickened,
pour it over the crabs. Sprinkle over all the slivered almonds, and serve.

LOBSTERS

The answer to the question, "When is a lobster not a lobster?" is "When it's a crayfish."

The true lobster is found only in the waters of the North and Middle Atlantic. It has five pairs of legs, of which the first two are enormous pincers, or claws. One is heavier than the other, with blunt teeth, and is called a crusher. The smaller is called a cutter.

The crayfish, also known as the spiny lobster, and rock lobster, closely resembles the true lobster, but it does not have the two large pincer claws. The edible meat is all in its tail. The French name for this crustacean is *Langouste*. The best known market name is frozen rock lobster tails.

As previously mentioned, lobsters should be alive up to the moment of cooking. When ready to prepare, cross the large claws of the lobster and hold them firmly with the left hand. Then insert a large, sharp knife into the back between the body and tail shells. This kills the lobster instantly by severing the spinal cord. Then place the lobster on its back and split it open from head to tail. Remove the small sac back of the head (the stomach) and the black vein running from head to tail (the intestinal tract). The lobster is then ready for cooking.

If you should rebel at this method, fill a large kettle with cool water. Place the lobster in it, and let it come gently to a boil.

The following recipe was reputedly created for Napoleon Bonaparte. It was apparently first served to the Emperor sometime between July 19 and August 17, because that period was the eleventh month in the calendar of the First Republic and was called Thermidor.

LOBSTER THERMIDOR

2 1½-lb. lobsters	¾ cup milk
4 tbsp. olive oil	¼ cup cream

1 medium-sized onion	2 tbsp. dry mustard
1 cup sliced fresh	Pinch paprika
mushrooms	2 tbsp. grated Parmesan
2 tbsp. butter	cheese
2 tbsp. flour	⅔ cup sherry
¼ tsp. salt	Bread crumbs
Pinch cayenne pepper	Additional butter

Split 2 1½-pound lobsters, removing the sac at the back of the head.

Put 4 tablespoons of olive oil in a large pan, heat it, and then put the lobsters in, split side down. Cover and cook slowly for about 10 to 12 minutes. Remove the lobsters from the pan, remove the meat from the bodies and claws, reserving the shells, which should be kept warm.

To the oil the lobsters were sautéed in (adding a little more, if necessary), add one medium-sized onion, peeled and chopped, and 1 cup of sliced fresh mushrooms. Let this cook until tender.

In another pan melt 2 tablespoons of butter over a medium flame. Stir in 2 tablespoons of flour, ¼ teaspoon salt, and a pinch of cayenne pepper, and when smooth, add ¾ cup of milk. Stir over the fire until mixture comes to a boil. Then add this mixture to the mushroom and onion mixture, together with ¼ cup of cream, 2 tablespoons of dry mustard, a pinch of paprika, and 2 tablespoons of grated Parmesan cheese. Reduce this whole mixture to a thick creamy consistency with about ⅔ cup of sherry. Stir the cut-up lobster meat into the sauce and stuff the lobster shells with the mixture. Sprinkle the tops of the lobsters with bread crumbs, dot with butter, and put under the broiler to brown. Then serve.

I don't suppose, among the elite, there is a better known dish than Lobster à la Newburg. In the gay 90's this dish was practically a "must" at gay after-theater parties. I remember chuckling over a remark of a perky old *boulevardier* in New York when he was recounting some of his past escapades. "In private dining rooms and bachelor apartments Lobster à la Newburg served in a chafing dish and an iced bottle of champagne were considered to be the perfect prelude to a seduction."

During the Civil War one of the well-known men-about-town in New York was a chap by the name of Ben Wenburg, whose favorite eating place was Delmonico's. He was very fond of gathering a group of friends together and preparing his own special lobster dish, which was boiled lobster served in a creamy, aromatic sauce. In honor of his wealthy patron Delmonico named this dish Lobster à la Wenburg, and it became a specialty of that famous restaurant. Sometime later, however, Delmonico and Wenburg quarreled, and in retaliation Delmonico reversed the first three letters of his former patron's now odious name and called it Lobster à la Newburg.

There are a great many recipes for Lobster à la Newburg, and they are to be found in a great many cookbooks, but I have developed a slight variation. I brazenly call the following recipe Lobster Newburg à la Wood, and I think all of your taste buds will have a rousing convention when you taste it.

LOBSTER NEWBURG À LA WOOD

4 oz. butter	3 cups cooked lobster meat
1 tbsp. chopped parsley	2 oz. brandy
3 tbsp. flour	¼ tsp. Worcestershire
1 tbsp. grated onion	sauce
Dash Angostura bitters	Salt
¼ tsp. dry mustard	Freshly ground pepper
Dash paprika	2 oz. dry Madeira wine
Pinch cayenne pepper	½ lemon, juice of
1 cup cream	1 tbsp. butter
1 tbsp. flour	

In the top of a double boiler over gently boiling water in the lower half melt 2 ounces of butter, add the chopped parsley, and 3 tablespoons of flour. Stir the flour in slowly so that no lumps develop. Then add the grated onion, Angostura bitters, mustard, paprika, and cayenne pepper, and stir well. Then slowly add the cream, and again blend well.

In a saucepan melt 2 ounces of butter, and when it is hot add the lobster meat, cut in fairly large dice. Then pour over the lobster meat the brandy, which has been warmed. Set the whole alight, and let the flame die out.

Add the lobster meat and the juices from the saucepan to the cream sauce in the top of the double boiler. Also add the Worcestershire sauce and salt and freshly ground pepper to taste, and stir well. Then add the dry Madeira wine and the lemon juice.

Make a *roux* of 1 tablespoon of butter and 1 tablespoon of flour, and when blended stir the *roux* into the lobster and sauce mixture. Again blend everything well, and allow to heat for about 5 minutes. Serve over buttered toast, buttered English muffin halves, or Melba toast.

To make this in a chafing dish, make the sauce in the blazer pan placed in the outer pan, in which there is water. The lobster meat can be prepared in a saucepan (use that beautiful Revere Ware with the copper bottom) and brought to the table. Then pour the brandy over it, set it alight, and when the flame has died out, pour the contents of the saucepan into the sauce heating in the blazer pan. Continue on from there with the following recipe steps.

OYSTERS

Oysters are very versatile little mollusks. They fit into all sorts of menus, from breakfast (creamed oysters on waffles are delicious) to midnight suppers, and they can be combined with almost any sort of food. Many gourmets think it a sin to cook oysters, while others prefer them cooked to raw. Oysters are adaptable to any method of cooking, and they are very healthy, containing generous amount of vitamins A, B, C, and D. To the ancient Romans oysters were the "dainty manna of the sea," the crowning touch to a banquet.

The myth about oysters not being edible during the months without an "r" in them has long been exploded. In these days of modern refrigeration there is little danger of spoilage. However, during the "r-less" months oysters are breeding, and are very active eaters when the water is warm. Therefore, they are not as tasty during the summer.

I must offer one tip to readers. In visiting the Northern Pacific coast, don't fail to sample the tiny Olympia oysters. They are the quintessence of succulence.

One of the most celebrated oyster dishes is Oysters Rockefeller, which is said to have originated many years ago in Antoine's, the famous New Orleans restaurant. According to the legend, the guests to whom it was served exclaimed, "This is as rich as Rockefeller." And so it was appropriately named Oysters Rockefeller. The recipe is supposed to be a deep, dark secret which utilizes eighteen ingredients. This one contains only twelve, but for my money it can't be improved upon.

OYSTERS ROCKEFELLER

3 *dozen large oysters on half shell*
1 *cup minced raw spinach*
6 *little green onions*
¼ *cup minced parsley*
¼ *cup minced celery leaves*
¼ *tsp. tarragon*
¼ *tsp. chervil*
Dash Tabasco
Salt
Pepper
½ *cup buttered bread crumbs*
1 *tbsp. Herbsaint or Pernod*
½ *cup sweet butter*

Put through a food chopper, using the finest blade, washed spinach leaves separated from their stems, 6 little green onions, celery leaves and parsley, so that you come out with the amounts indicated above. It wouldn't do any harm to put the above ingredients through the food chopper a second time. Sprinkle into the chopped ingredients ¼ teaspoon each of tarragon and chervil, a dash of Tabasco, salt and freshly ground black pepper to taste. Then mix in ½ cup of fine bread crumbs, which have been browned in a little butter, and add 1 tablespoon of Herbsaint or Pernod, which are absinthe substitutes.

If, by any chance, you are the fortunate possessor of some real absinthe (which is no longer permitted to be manufactured), use it, of course. Next, work in ½ cup of sweet (unsalted) butter into the mixture, and knead thoroughly. This is the paste that makes the sauce.

Place 3 dozen large raw oysters on the half shell in a baking pan, or pie tins, filled almost to the brim with rock salt (that's the kind you used in an ice-cream freezer, remember?). Place in a preheated 400-degree oven for about 5 minutes, or until the edges of the oysters begin to curl. Then place a full tablespoon of the sauce over each oyster, return them to the hot oven for about another 5 minutes, and serve immediately.

Oysters Casino also call for oysters on the half shell, but they are broiled.

OYSTERS CASINO

24 *oysters on half shell* *	*Salt and pepper*
2 *slices lean bacon, diced*	1 *chopped pimento*
2 *tbsp. butter*	1 *tsp. dry sherry*
1 *small onion, minced*	*Dash Worcestershire sauce*
½ *green pepper, minced*	*Few drops lemon juice*

See that the oysters and their shells are free from sand and clean.

Place the diced bacon in a skillet, and fry slowly over a low flame until crisp—about 3 minutes.

In a saucepan melt the butter over a medium flame, and add the minced onion and green pepper, and salt and pepper to taste. Sauté for about 5 minutes, or until the vegetables are tender. Then pour the contents of the saucepan into the skillet with the diced bacon, and add the chopped pimento, dry sherry, dash of Worcestershire sauce, and a few drops of lemon juice. Mix everything well.

* In place of the half-shell service, distribute the oysters equally on 4 toasted half slices of English muffins, which have been spread with mayonnaise, place in a buttered shallow baking dish, and cover with the sauce. Place under the broiler, 3 inches from the flame, and broil for 3 minutes. Serve on individual hot plates.

Cover the oysters in their half shells with the above mixture, distributing it evenly over the oysters. Bed the oysters in their half shells in rock salt on a cookie sheet or in pans, and place under the broiler, 3 inches from the flame, and broil for 3 minutes. This serves 4.

The following gastronomic masterpiece—fried oysters served in a hollowed-out loaf of French bread—is not only delicious, but has a cute connotation. Some people call it Oyster Loaf, but I much prefer the Creole designation, *La Mediatrice,* which translated means "the peacemaker."

LA MEDIATRICE

1 *unsliced loaf of French bread*	1 *tsp. sherry*
	Salt
2 *dozen oysters*	Pepper
Flour	Yellow corn meal
Beaten yolk of one egg	Fat
Slivers of dill pickle	

Cut off the top of an entire loaf of French bread and scoop out the inside to make a basket, leaving about ½ inch of crust all around. Toast the basket and the lid, butter them generously, and keep them warm.

Dip the oysters first in flour, then in the beaten egg yolk, which has been seasoned with salt and pepper and a teaspoon of sherry, and finally dip them in the yellow corn meal. Then fry the oysters in hot fat until brown. Remove them from the fat and drain, and then place them in the toasted loaf. Lay thin slivers of dill pickles over the oysters, place the lid on top and pop the loaf into the oven to get thoroughly warm.

In the galaxy of cooked oyster dishes I don't know of one that is more succulent, more satisfying to the appetite, or that leaves you with a warmer glow of contentment than an oyster stew.

I am not speaking of the skimmed-milk-and-tough-bivalve concoction that one encounters all too often in various eateries. I mean a rich, steaming bowl of oyster stew that intrigues your eyes as its fragrance impels your taste buds to do nip ups.

One of the best oyster stews I have ever eaten in a restaurant was served to me in the Oyster Bar of the Grand Central Terminal in New York City. But even that masterly concoction runs a poor second to the following recipe, which you can easily make in your own home.

OYSTER STEW, M.W.

3 *pints oysters*	1 *bay leaf*
4 *tbsp. butter*	1 *tsp. salt*
1 *clove garlic*	⅛ *tsp. white pepper*
2 *medium onions, minced*	*Dash cayenne pepper*
2½ *cups milk*	½ *cup dry white wine*
2½ *cups cream*	*Chopped parsley*
½ *cup chopped celery tops*	*Paprika*

In a saucepan lightly brown the crushed clove of garlic and the minced onions in 3 tablespoons of butter. Then discard the garlic.

Put the milk and the cream in the top of a double boiler to heat over gently boiling water in the lower part. Then add the cooked onions and the butter they were cooked in, the chopped celery tops, bay leaf, and 1 pint of oysters which have been coarsely chopped (the remaining 2 pints should not be chopped, but left whole). Mix all, and let this heat for about 20 minutes, but do not allow to boil. Then strain the mixture through a fine sieve, discarding the solids, and return the strained liquid to the top of the double boiler.

In a saucepan put the remaining 2 pints of whole oysters (and their liquor, if they are bulk oysters) to heat, together with the salt, white pepper, and cayenne pepper. Just as the edges of the oysters begin to curl, add them and their liquor to the strained milk and cream. Also add the remaining 1 tablespoon of butter and stir in the dry white wine. Cook for a minute or two longer, or until the mixture is thoroughly heated. Serve in heated bowls, with a sprinkling of chopped parsley over the top, and a dusting of paprika. This may serve 6, but you'd be safer in figuring on 4.

SCALLOPS

I suppose every American visitor to Paris has, at one time or another, eaten *Coquille Saint Jacques*, one of the glories of French cuisine. However, there is no reason why you can't duplicate this dish, made with scallops, right in your own home in the authentic French manner. But here's a word of advice. Try to get small, or bay, scallops—the large sea scallops are far less delicate and they have to be cut into halves or quarters.

COQUILLE SAINT JACQUES
(Scallops)

2 *lb. fresh scallops*	*Freshly ground pepper*
1 *pint dry white wine*	*Pinch thyme*
Salt	*Pinch marjoram*
4 *tbsp. butter*	1½ *tbsp. flour*
1 *cup sliced mushrooms*	*Rich cream*
4 *little green onions*	*Fine bread crumbs*
1 *tbsp. minced parsley*	*Paprika*

Heat 1 pint of dry California white wine, and add 2 pounds of washed fresh scallops along with a pinch of salt. Simmer for about 10 minutes. When the scallops become very white, drain them, reserving the liquid. Keep the scallops warm.

In a saucepan melt 4 tablespoons of butter, then add 1 cup of sliced fresh mushrooms, 4 little green onions, chopped, 1 tablespoon of minced parsley, salt and freshly ground pepper to taste, and a pinch each of marjoram and thyme. When the mushrooms and onions are tender, add about 1½ tablespoons of flour and stir until smooth. Then slowly pour in the warm scallop broth (wine). Add enough rich cream—about 2 tablespoons—to thicken the sauce (it must not be thin). Now add a pinch of paprika and the scallops, each cut into 2 or 4 pieces, depending on the size. After blending the whole over a low flame, cool slightly, and then fill buttered scallop shells with the mixture, which should be heavy enough to form a neat mold. Sprinkle a few fine breadcrumbs over each mound, dot with butter, and place under the broiler flame. Cook until the crust is golden brown.

SHRIMP

Probably the most popular crustacean is the shrimp. Incidentally, there is no difference between *prawns,* which the English call them, *scampi,* which is the Italian designation, and the American shrimp, except for size. The former two are merely larger. However, large shrimps caught off the Louisiana coast are often designated as "jumbo Louisiana prawns."

There is another species of shrimp that I must mention—the Bay shrimp, or, to give it its official name, *Crago franciscorum.* There are only two places in the world where it is to be found—on the Northern Pacific coast, and in the Morcombe Bay in Cornwall, England. It is tiny, and when shelled, there is only about 1 inch of meat remaining. But what an inch of sweet and luscious succulence!

By the way, if you want a new taste thrill, boil shrimps in 3 parts stale beer and 1 part water, to which have been added a few peppercorns, a bay leaf or two, salt, and a sprinkling of celery seeds. Allow to cool, then eat as is.

One of the most delightful shrimp dishes I ever ate was served in the home of Walt Newton, a well-known announcer on the Mutual Broadcasting System. Walt, a Texan, is an excellent host, and instead of lounging in the living room while his better half slaved over a hot stove, he donned an apron and invited us into the kitchen, where he set about preparing what he calls Shrimps Jubalai.

SHRIMPS JUBALAI

2 lb. fresh shrimps	4 bay leaves
2 tbsp. peanut oil	1 tsp. thyme
3 medium-sized onions	2 tsp. chili powder
3 small cloves garlic	Salt
8 stalks Pascal celery	Pepper
1 green pepper	1 4-oz. can mushrooms
1 #2½ can tomatoes	1 small can pimentos
	boiled rice

Into a fairly large skillet with a close-fitting cover put 2 tablespoons of peanut oil (a salad oil may be used, but it's not as good). When the oil is hot, add 3 medium-sized onions, chopped, and 3 small cloves of garlic, peeled and sliced. When the onions are yellow and tender, add ¾ of the chopped celery (including all the leaves). Next, put into the mixture 1 chopped green pepper, and cook over a medium flame for 5 minutes. Now put into the mixture a #2½ can of tomatoes, along with 4 bay leaves, 1 teaspoon thyme, 2 teaspoons of chili powder, and salt and pepper to taste. Put the lid on the skillet, and let everything cook for 10 minutes.

Next add to the mixture 2 pounds of washed and shelled shrimp, and the contents of both a 4-ounce can of mushrooms, and a small can of pimentos. Cook for about 7 minutes. Then add the remainder of the chopped celery and cook for about 3 minutes longer. This adds the final "Chinese touch," in that the bits of celery, cooking for only 3 minutes, remain crunchy and tasty.

Serve Shrimps Jubalai over flaky boiled rice (1½ cups uncooked).

If you've come home some night and found you've forgotten to order meat and you have some canned shrimp on the pantry shelf, try Shrimps de Jonghe. It's easy to make if you follow this original recipe from the once famous Chicago restaurant of the same name. Of course, this dish is even better if fresh shrimps are used.

SHRIMPS DE JONGHE

3 lb. cooked shrimps	Pinch tarragon
1 large clove garlic	Pinch marjoram
¾ cup butter	1 cup fine bread crumbs
1 tsp. salt	½ cup dry sherry
	Chopped parsley

Mash 1 large clove of garlic until it is almost a paste, then add to it ¾ cup of butter, softened to room temperature, 1 teaspoon salt, and 1 pinch each of tarragon and marjoram. Cream these together until well blended, then add 1 cup of fine bread crumbs and ½ cup of dry sherry. Blend the whole well.

For six people have 3 pounds of cooked shrimps. In a fairly large buttered baking dish place alternate layers of the shrimps and the bread crumb mixture, sprinkling chopped parsley over the top of each layer. Bake in a 400-degree oven for 20 to 25 minutes, and serve immediately.

One of my favorite types of food is curry. Almost every type of shellfish can be made into a curry. I think the finest shellfish curries I have ever eaten were made the way curry is prepared and cooked in Penang, the town and island which, after Singapore, forms the most important part of the British Crown Colony of Straits Settlements.

EAST INDIAN SHRIMP CURRY

2 lb. fresh boiled shrimps	Pinch dried mint
4 oz. butter	2 cloves
1 clove garlic	¼ tsp. basil
1 large onion	2 tbsp. flour
3 stalks celery	2 tbsp. curry powder
1 green pepper	½ tsp. salt
1 apple	½ tsp. pepper
1 carrot	¼ tsp. cayenne pepper

2 tomatoes

1 tbsp. chopped parsley

1 bay leaf

Pinch thyme

Pinch marjoram

¼ tsp. nutmeg

2 cups consommé

1 cup dry white wine

Boiled rice

Chutney

Melt 4 ounces of butter in a large saucepan, and add 1 clove of garlic, crushed; 1 large onion, peeled and chopped fine; 3 stalks of celery, chopped; 1 green pepper, seeded and chopped; 1 apple peeled, cored, and chopped; 1 carrot, chopped; 2 tomatoes, peeled, seeded, and chopped; 1 tablespoon chopped parsley; 1 crumbled bay leaf; a pinch each of thyme, marjoram, and dried mint; 2 whole cloves; and ¼ teaspoon basil. When the vegetables are soft, sprinkle in 2 tablespoons of flour mixed with 2 tablespoons curry powder, ½ teaspoon salt, ½ teaspoon freshly ground pepper, ¼ teaspoon cayenne pepper, and ¼ teaspoon nutmeg. Mix well with the contents of the pan, stirring well, and cook for about 5 minutes. Then slowly add 2 cups of consommé, and when the mixture begins to thicken, add 1 cup of dry California white wine. Cook over a slow fire for about ½ hour.

Now you can do one of two things. If you like a thin curry sauce, you can strain the above mixture into another saucepan, add 2 pounds of freshly boiled shrimps, shelled and cleaned. Simmer for about 10 minutes. On a platter have a ring of 1 cup of raw rice which has been boiled, and pour the shrimp curry into the center of the ring. Sprinkle with finely chopped parsley, and serve with chutney.

Your second choice is to add the shrimps to the sauce without straining it, let heat, and serve on individual plates over a mound of fluffy rice. Of course, chutney is also indicated in both methods. Personally, I prefer this latter method.

6. MEAT

Some hae meat, and canna eat,
And some wad eat that want it;
But we hae meat, and we can eat,
And sae the Lord be thankit.

Robert Burns.

Meat is recognized as one of the most important foods in our diet (and I don't mean reducing!). Therefore most menus today are built around meat of some sort. And there are reasons for this. First and foremost, meat is appetizing and flavorsome, and may be had in a large variety. Equally important, meat supplies in abundance energy, vitamins, minerals, and fatty acids.

Many people think that gourmet meat dishes are limited to expensive cuts that are either broiled or roasted: steaks, chops, fillets, prime ribs, or loins. But the fact is that some of the great gastronomic masterpieces utilizing meat are basically stews. They were not devised by master chefs in the grand manner of *haute cuisine*. Nearly all of them are regional dishes that originated in peasant kitchens, calling for comestibles that are inexpensive and plentiful.

Almost any fine basic cookbook, particulary those dealing with meat, will give you all the information you will ever need about the various cuts of meat and the best method of the preparation of each, and about the various methods of cooking meat.

It is an old saying that "a bottle of Burgundy, a ragout and a beautiful and intelligent woman are the three best table companions possible to find."

Of course, there are bound to be differences of opinions as to the beautiful and intelligent woman. One person might perfer an intellectual brunette, another a witty blonde, and still another a philosophical redhead. But there can be no difference of opinion on the ragout, *Boeuf Bourguignon*.

The real *Boeuf Bourguignon* is simply Burgundy Beef, or beef stewed in Burgundy. The only extraneous flavors which mingle with it are onions, which have already been cooked, set aside, and added later, and the delicate flavor of mushrooms.

This delectable dish is really a very simple one to cook. Get yourself a couple of bottles of good Burgundy (Romanée Conti is practically impossible to get in America, so, depending on the state of your pocketbook, try either Chambertin or Vougeot from France, or Pinot Noir from California), your favorite feminine or masculine companion, and two pounds of lean beef (chuck is the best), and I'll guarantee you an evening that you'll not forget very soon. It's really as easy as that . . . and this.

BOEUF BOURGUIGNON
(Burgundy Beef)

½ cup beef bouillon	10 *small or* 5 *medium-sized*
1 cup dry red wine	*onions*
½ pound fresh mushrooms	Marjoram
2 lb. lean beef	Thyme
2 tbsp. bacon drippings	Salt
1½ tbsp. flour	Pepper

Peel and slice the onions and fry them in the bacon drippings until brown, using a heavy skillet. Then remove to a separate dish. Cut the lean beef into about 1-inch cubes, and sauté them in the same drippings, adding a little more fat if necessary. When the cubes of beef are browned on all sides, sprinkle over them 1½ tablespoons of flour, and a generous pinch each of salt, pepper, marjoram, and thyme. Then add ½ cup of beef bouillon to the contents of the skillet, and 1 cup of red wine (don't use your imported wine for this; rather, a good California Burgundy). Stir the mixture well for a moment, then let it simmer as slowly as possible for 3¼ hours. The mixture, during this cooking, should just barely bubble occasionally. If necessary, put a mat under the skillet. The liquid may cook away some, so add a little more bouillon and wine (in the proportion of one part of stock to two parts of wine) as necessary to keep the beef barely covered.

After the mixture has cooked the 3¼ hours, return the brown onions to the skillet, add ½ pound of sliced fresh mushrooms (you can add ¾ of a pound or a pound if you like mushrooms). Stir everything together well, and then let it cook for ¾ of an hour or even an hour longer. Again, it may be necessary to add a little more stock and wine. The sauce should be thick and dark brown. With this main dish serve crusty French bread, a tossed green salad, and your imported Burgundy, and follow it with a light dessert.

To my mind the most elegant, and one of the most delicious beef dishes is broiled tenderloin of beef, or fillet of beef, as it is also called, with a mushroom sauce. This is a dish that is literally "fit for a king," and is an ideal entree for a party of ten or twelve. Of course the fillet, or tenderloin, is the most tender cut of beef that can be had, and if it comes from prime or choice beef its flavor and texture are unsurpassed. The whole tenderloin will weigh between five and six pounds, and it is broiled whole. When you buy it, have your butcher remove all of the fat and trim it, and then lard it well. Also have him grind the trimmings, which you will use in the sauce.

The best procedure, I think, is to make the sauce first. It can be started a little while before you put the tenderloin under the broiler, or it can be made a little in advance. But it must always be kept hot, because it must be instantly available the moment the tenderloin is removed from the broiler.

BROILED BEEF TENDERLOIN, MUSHROOM SAUCE

1 *beef tenderloin, 5-6 lbs.*	3 *oz. butter*
½ *lb. fresh mushrooms, sliced*	1 *large clove garlic*
Ground trimmings from meat	2 *medium onions, sliced*
1 *tbsp. Escoffier Sauce Diable*	2 *tbsp. chili sauce*
Pinch hickory smoked salt	*Pinch dried marjoram*
2 *dashes Worcestershire sauce*	*Pinch dried thyme*
5 *oz. dry red wine*	4 *drops Tabasco sauce*
2 *oz. condensed beef bouillon*	*Salt and pepper*
½ *tsp. flour*	

For the sauce, melt the butter in a fairly large skillet. Peel a large clove of garlic and cut it lengthwise into slivers. Put these slivers into the hot butter, and add the sliced fresh mushrooms and the onions, sliced. Sauté for about 5 minutes, or until the onions are limp. Then add the ground trimmings from the tenderloin (or about ¼ pound of ground hamburger), and break up the meat with a fork, stirring constantly. At the end of about 4 or 5 minutes add the chili sauce, Sauce Diable, the dried marjoram and thyme, a generous pinch of the hickory smoked salt, the Tabasco sauce, Worcestershire sauce, dry red wine, beef bouillon, a sprinkling of salt and pepper, and the flour. Stir this mixture well, and let it just barely simmer until ready to pour over the tenderloin when it is put in a roaster.

To cook the tenderloin, preheat the oven for 15 minutes, with the broiling pan in, at 550 degrees. Also have your beef tenderloin at room temperature. Put the larded tenderloin on the broiling pan, not more than 2 inches from the flame or heat units, and cook under the broiler at its highest heat for 8 minutes. Then turn the tenderloin and cook for about 7 minutes on the other side. Then take it from under the broiler and place it in a roaster, pour the sauce over it, and put it in a 350-

degree oven for about 10 minutes. Remove the tenderloin to a hot platter, pour the sauce over it, and serve.

Remember, one of the greatest culinary crimes is to overcook a tenderloin of beef. When it is sliced the center should be definitely pink, shading to a crisply done outside.

Fine steaks should be broiled. I always allow a steak to stand at room temperature for about an hour before broiling, after first having rubbed the finest olive oil into both sides of the steak. Then I put it under the broiler, the top of the steak about 2 to 2½ inches from the flame. Depending upon thickness, I let it broil about 6 minutes (for a steak 1½ inches thick). Then I salt and pepper it, and turn it over and broil the other side for about 4 to 5 minutes (this leaves the steak well browned outside, and a little pink on the inside—rare, but not raw). That side is salted and peppered, generously dotted with butter, and served on a hot platter.

The following recipe will give you what I and my wife consider the most luscious steak we have ever tasted.

PIQUANT BROILED STEAK

1 *porterhouse steak*, 1½ *inches thick*	Garlic powder
	Worcestershire sauce
Olive oil	*Soft butter*
Minced fresh ginger root	*Dry mustard*
Hickory smoked salt	*Freshly ground pepper*
Paprika	

Rub olive oil into both sides of the steak, and allow to stand at room temperature for at least an hour. Just before broiling, sprinkle one side of the steak with finely minced fresh ginger root.

Place the steak under the broiler, with the side sprinkled with the ginger root up. Broil for about 6 minutes. Then sprinkle with hickory smoked salt, freshly ground pepper, and a pinch of garlic powder. Then turn the steak, sprinkle the uncooked side with minced fresh ginger root, and broil for about 4 to 4½ minutes (if you want to test the doneness of a steak, cut a small gash with a sharp knife along the edge of the bone, bend the meat back, and note its color. Do this after about 4 minutes of broiling the second side. If there is any rawness visible, let⁻ it cook for about ½ to 1 minute more). When the second side is finished, repeat the seasoning of the first side. Then remove the steak to a hot platter.

Cover the top with 1 to 2 tablespoons of soft butter, sprinkle over the top a generous pinch (about ½ teaspoon) of dry mustard, a generous sprinkling of Worcestershire sauce (about 1 teaspoon), and a sprinkling of paprika. Then turn the steak over, and follow the same procedure on the other side, and serve.

This is really not saucing the steak; rather, it is a seasoning. When you slice the steak (I usually remove the T-shaped bone from the steak with a sharp knife the moment it is on the platter) the juices of the steak mingle with the butter-mustard-Worcestershire-paprika seasoning (which I spoon over each serving), and you get the wonderful flavor of the meat, which is enhanced by the marvelous piquancy of the seasoned juices.

The second broiled steak recipe with a sauce is a Piquant Paste which, incidentally, is a favorite of Joan Crawford's.

BROILED STEAK WITH PIQUANT PASTE

1 steak	2 tbsp. Madeira
4 tbsp. Roquefort or blue cheese	Dash Tabasco
	Juice ½ lemon
1 tbsp. butter	Salt
1 tbsp. scraped onion pulp	Freshly ground pepper

Make the piquant paste as follows: Mix together 4 tablespoons of Roquefort (or blue) cheese, 1 tablespoon of butter, 1 tablespoon of scraped onion pulp, 2 tablespoons of Madeira, a dash of Tabasco, the juice of ½ lemon, and salt and freshly ground pepper to taste. Broil 1½- or 2-inch steak in whatever way you prefer, rare or medium rare. When it is done, spread the paste over it (on top side only) and put it under the broiler for about 10 seconds, then serve immediately.

There is scarcely any Russian restaurant of repute that doesn't feature Beef Stroganoff on its menu, and you'll often find it on the menu of other very fine restaurants. It was named, I am told, for a Russian gay blade and gourmet, Count Paul Stroganoff, but whether it was a concoction of his own or of his chef I have never known. But it is one of the most taste-teasing beef dishes ever devised, and it never fails to bring exclamations of delight from guests. There are many variations of Beef Stroganoff, but I think this one is tops.

BEEF STROGANOFF

1½ lb. lean beef	2 cups beef bouillon or con-
3 tbsp. butter	sommé
1 cup sliced fresh mush-	2 tbsp. tomato paste
rooms	1 tsp. dry mustard
1 large onion	3 tbsp. sherry
2 tbsp. flour	⅔ cup sour cream

Get 1½ pounds lean beef, remove all the fat and gristle from it, and cut it into narrow strips about 2½ inches long, ¾ inch wide, and between ¼ and ½ inch thick. Dust the strips with salt and pepper and set them aside for about 2 hours, but not in the refrigerator or other cold place. When you are ready to prepare the dish, melt 2 tablespoons of butter in a heavy skillet, and sauté 1 cup of sliced fresh mushrooms until tender (about 15 minutes), then remove them and set them aside. In the same butter sauté the peeled and sliced onion until brown, then remove and set aside. Add at least one tablespoon of butter to the skillet, and when it is bubbling hot put in the strips of beef and sear them on both sides, but leave them rare. Remove them and set them aside, and to the remaining butter in the skillet sprinkle in 2 tablespoons of flour and blend it with the butter, browning it well. Then slowly add 2 cups of beef bouillon (or consommé), stirring well to form a smooth gravy. Next add 3 tablespoons of sherry, 2 tablespoons of tomato paste, and 1 teaspoon of dry mustard, blending them well. Now put into the sauce the meat, onions, and mushrooms, and let the whole thing simmer very slowly over the lowest possible flame for about 20 minutes. About 5 minutes before serving add ⅔ cup of sour cream and blend it in thoroughly. Whipped or riced potatoes make an ideal accompaniment to the dish.

A pot roast, properly prepared, is a mighty fine dish. It is full of flavor, and its fairly long cooking renders it tender. One of the most famous pot roasts is the German *Sauerbraten,* which is really spiced beef. For all pot roasts the top or bottom round is excellent, also pieces from the rump, chuck, or neck. About 4 pounds, all in one piece, will serve anywhere from 4 to 6 people, depending upon their appetites, and what other foods are served with the meal.

The following recipe for pot roast is of my own devising, and I can guarantee its enticing flavor.

POT ROAST OF BEEF WITH BRANDY

4 lbs. beef, in one piece	1 tsp. pepper
Brandy	2 medium-sized onions, sliced
2 small cloves garlic	
Salt	4 medium-sized carrots, quartered
Freshly ground pepper	
Flour	½ cup chopped celery
2 tbsp. bacon drippings	2 fresh tomatoes, sliced
2 tbsp. olive oil	1 cup dry red wine
4 tbsp. brandy	½ lb. sliced fresh mushrooms
1 bay leaf	
Pinch dried thyme	2 oz. butter
Pinch dried marjoram	½ cup sour cream
1 tsp. salt	2 tbsp. flour
2 tbsp. butter	

Wipe a 4-pound piece of beef, preferably cut from the

top of the round, with a cloth dampened with brandy.
Then quarter the cloves of garlic, make small incisions
in the top of the meat, and insert the garlic slivers in
them. Then sprinkle the meat on all sides with seasoned
flour, patting it into the meat.

In a heavy iron kettle melt the bacon drippings and
add the olive oil. When hot, put in the meat and sear it
well on all sides until nicely browned. Then pour over
the meat in the kettle 4 tablespoons of brandy, and set
it alight. (CAUTION: turn out the flame under the kettle, and be sure the kettle is not under anything, because the flame will mount about a foot above the kettle.)
Let the brandy blaze until the flame dies down, and then
extinguish it with the top of the kettle.

Put the kettle back over the flame, and add the bay
leaf, crumbled, the pinches of dried thyme and marjoram, salt and pepper, the onions, sliced, the carrots,
quartered lengthwise, the chopped celery, the tomatoes,
sliced, and the dry red wine. Place a tight-fitting lid on
the kettle, and let the contents simmer slowly for 3½ to
4 hours.

When the cooking time has elapsed, remove the meat
to a hot platter and, with a slotted spoon, remove the
vegetables, spooning them on top of the meat. Place the
platter in a warm oven and proceed to make the gravy.

Sauté the sliced fresh mushrooms in the butter in a
skillet. When they are tender (about 6 minutes), put
them into the gravy in the kettle. Also add the sour
cream. Make a *roux* of the 2 tablespoons each of butter
and flour, and add this *roux* to the gravy, stirring and
blending well until smooth. Allow the gravy to cook
briskly until thickened and smooth, then pour it into a
gravy boat or tureen.

Serve buttered noodles with the pot roast, and slice
the beef, including in each portion some of the vegetables.
Pour the gravy over the meat, and the noodles too, if
you like it that way.

A tossed green salad goes excellently with the entree,
particularly if it has a blue cheese or Roquefort dressing.
The same wine that went into the pot roast should be

served with the dinner. A dessert suggestion? Cherry pie and coffee.

Let's take a little gastronomical tour, starting in London with beefsteak and kidney pie.

In the famous old Cheshire Cheese in London the steak and kidney pie was out of this world. It's not a difficult dish to make and, naturally, should be washed down with Bass's ale or Guinness's stout, or your favorite American ale or beer.

BEEFSTEAK AND KIDNEY PIE

1 *lb. veal kidneys*	1 *bay leaf*
Salt	1 *tbsp. Worcestershire sauce*
Vinegar	*Freshly ground pepper*
2 *lb. rump steak*	1 *cup beef bouillon*
Flour	1 *cup dry red wine*
1 *clove garlic*	3 *tbsp. butter*
3 *tbsp. bacon fat*	1 *cup sliced mushrooms*
1 *medium-sized onion*	3 *oz. brandy*
2 *pinches thyme*	*Pastry crust*
2 *pinches marjoram*	*Cream*

Soak 1 pound of veal kidneys for an hour in cold salted water to which 2 tablespoons of vinegar have been added. Then drain the kidneys, clean, trim away any gristle and tubes, and slice them thin.

Cut 2 pounds of ½-inch-thick rump steak into 1- by 1½-inch pieces.

In a Dutch oven sauté 1 clove of sliced garlic until brown in 3 tablespoons of bacon drippings. Remove the garlic and add the cubed beef which has been dredged with flour. Brown the meat on all sides, then add 1 medium-sized onion, peeled and chopped fine, 2 pinches each of thyme and marjoram, a crumbled bay leaf, 1 tablespoon of Worcestershire sauce, and salt and freshly ground pepper to taste. Cook for about 5 minutes, then add 1 cup of beef bouillon and 1 cup of dry California red wine. Cover closely and simmer over a low flame for about 1½ hours, or until the meat is nearly tender. Stir occasionally, and, if necessary, add a little more bouillon and wine in equal parts.

In a saucepan put 1 tablespoon of butter, and when it is bubbling, add the sliced kidneys and cook for about 5 minutes, then add them to the simmering meat. Add about 2 more tablespoons of butter to the same pan, and put in 1 cup of sliced mushrooms. Sauté these gently for about 7 or 8 minutes, then add them to the simmering meat.

Now add 2 tablespoons of flour to the butter the kidneys and mushrooms have cooked in, and when well blended, add this *roux* to the simmering meat, kidneys, and mushrooms, and stir until well blended. Stir in 3 ounces of brandy, remove from the flame, pour all into a buttered casserole or a round baking dish, and set aside to cool.

Prepare a crust, to cover the top, according to your favorite recipe, or from prepared pie crust mix, and chill the dough in the refrigerator. Then roll out the rich pastry so that it is about an inch larger in diameter than the dish you are to cover. Press it down in a fluted edge around the rim of the dish. Cut a few little slits on the top to allow the steam to escape. Brush the top of the pastry crust with a little cream, and bake in a 450-degree oven for 15 minutes; then reduce the heat to about 300 degrees, and cook for 15 or 20 minutes longer. or until the pastry is a rich brown.

Well, next stop is Germany and the famous sweet-sour pot roast which is called *Sauerbraten*. This dish is a specialty in nearly all good German restaurants. It is not too difficult to prepare, but it does take time.

SAUERBRATEN

4 *lb. rump or round of beef*	1 *tsp. dry mustard*
(*1 piece*)	3 *bay leaves*
2½ *cups dry red wine*	12 *whole cloves*
1½ *cups tarragon vinegar*	2 *large onions*
1 *tsp. salt*	1 *carrot*
1 *tsp. black peppercorns*	6 *sprigs celery tops*

½ tsp. thyme   3 tbsp. bacon fat
½ tsp. mace   2 tbsp. flour
⅛ tsp. sage   5 gingersnaps
¼ tsp. allspice   1 cup sour cream
                2 tbsp. Madeira

Put a 4-pound rump or round of beef (in one piece) in a large enamel, earthenware, or stainless steel kettle. Mix together 2½ cups of dry American red wine, 1½ cups of tarragon vinegar, 1 teaspoon of salt, 1 teaspoon of black peppercorns, ½ teaspoon each of thyme and mace, ⅛ teaspoon of sage, ¼ teaspoon of allspice, 1 teaspoon of dry mustard, 3 bay leaves, 12 whole cloves, 2 large onions, peeled and sliced, 1 large carrot, sliced, and 6 sprigs celery tops. Pour this mixture over the meat. Cover with doubled cheesecloth, and let marinate for 4 days at room temperature, turning the meat twice each day in the marinade.

Melt 3 tablespoons of bacon drippings in a heavy frying pan or skillet, put in the meat, taken from the marinade, and brown it on all sides. Then put the meat into a heavy kettle or large Dutch oven.

Blend about 2 tablespoons of flour with the bacon drippings and gradually pour in the marinade, then add 5 crushed gingersnaps and cook until thickened. Add this sauce to the meat, cover, and simmer slowly over a low flame until the meat is tender—about 3 hours. If necessary, add a little more red wine.

When the meat is cooked, remove it to a hot platter and slice. Into the gravy stir 1 cup of sour cream and 2 tablespoons of Madeira. Heat, then pour the gravy over the meat, and serve.

Boeuf en daube came originally from the Provence section of France, I believe, and has been known for many centuries. It also is a great favorite in the Pyrenees, but it is made almost everywhere in France and is a great household stand-by in that country. It has a rather odd characteristic, in that it is equally delicious hot or cold. The cold version is said to have been perfected by Jean-Jacques Rousseau—the meat when cooked is put

in a bowl and the gravy, which is strained over it, will
set in a firm jelly when kept in a cold place.

In some localities, and especially among the Creoles of
Louisiana, a whole piece of beef, such as you would use
for a pot roast, is cooked as is. This method should be
used if you are going to serve it cold. If you've never
tried *boeuf en daube,* you'll find a new taste thrill from
it.

BOEUF EN DAUBE

3 lb. round of beef	1½ cups dry red wine
Salt	12 small white onions
Pepper	12 small carrots
Flour	6 whole peppercorns
6 strips bacon	4 whole cloves
2 cloves garlic	1 bay leaf
1 ounce brandy	2 tbsp. chopped parsley
12 small mushrooms	Pinch marjoram
1 cup beef bouillon	Pinch thyme

Cut 3 pounds of round of beef into about 1½ inch
pieces and roll in seasoned flour. Fry about 6 strips of
bacon in a heavy skillet. When they begin to brown, but
are not crisp, remove them and cut into 1-inch pieces,
and place in an earthenware casserole. In the fat in the
skillet, crush and chop finely 2 cloves of garlic, then put
in the floured pieces of beef and brown quickly on all
sides, turning frequently. When the pieces are browned,
pour 1 ounce of warm brandy into the skillet, and in a
few moments remove the meat to the casserole.

Now put about 12 small mushrooms into the skillet,
and when they are browned, transfer them to the casserole. Next add to the fat and the brandy in the skillet
1 cup of beef bouillon and 1 cup of California dry red
wine, preferably a claret type. Bring this to a boil, stirring
from the bottom of the pan to loosen all meat particles
that may adhere. Then pour the liquid in the skillet into
the casserole, over the beef, and add to the casserole
12 very small peeled white onions; 12 small carrots,
sliced; 6 peppercorns, slightly bruised; 4 whole cloves; a

crumbled bay leaf; 2 tablespoons of chopped parsley; and a generous pinch each of marjoram and thyme. Pour over the contents of the casserole another ½ cup of the dry red wine, and then cover the casserole tightly and bake in a 300-degree over for 3 hours. Serve from the casserole.

The Germans have a justly famous meatball dish which is, I believe, indigenous to East Prussia. But these meatballs are unlike any other meatballs that have been devised for the delight of the palate. Perhaps they might be likened to hamburgers, but they are boiled, not fried, and then they are simmered in a caper and sardellan sauce.

KÖNIGSBERGER KLOPS

¾ lb. chuck beef, ground
¾ lb. veal, ground
¼ lb. pork, ground
2 small hard rolls
½ cup light cream
1 medium onion, chopped
6 tbsp. butter
4 anchovy fillets
2 beaten eggs
1 tsp. salt

¼ tsp. freshly ground pepper
Lemon juice
2 tsp. Worcestershire sauce
2 tbsp. chopped parsley
¼ tsp. dried marjoram
5 cups beef bouillon
1 cup dry white wine
4 tbsp. flour
1 tsp. dry mustard
2 small boneless sardines

⅓ cup drained capers

Have the beef, veal, and pork ground twice. Also break up the hard rolls and soak them in the cream for about 10 minutes, then press the excess liquid from them. Also sauté the chopped onion in 1 tablespoon of butter until lightly browned.

Put the ground meats, the moistened hard rolls, the sautéed onions, and the anchovy fillets through the food grinder, using the finest blade. Then add to this the lightly beaten eggs, salt, freshly ground pepper, 1 tablespoon of lemon juice, the Worcestershire sauce, 1 tablespoon of chopped parsley, and the dried marjoram.

Mix everything thoroughly, and shape the mixture into 12 balls.

Heat the condensed beef bouillon and the dry white wine in a deep skillet or an iron kettle. When the liquid is boiling, carefully drop the meatballs in, turn down the flame, and simmer slowly for 15 to 20 minutes, covered. Then remove the meatballs from the stock, and keep them hot while the gravy is being made.

Mix the dry mustard with the flour, and cream that mixture together with 4 tablespoons of butter. When the *roux* is smooth, add enough of the hot stock the meatballs were boiled in to make a thin paste, free from lumps. Turn up the flame under the stock, then stir the *roux* into the stock. Cook and stir until smooth and boiling.

Mash the sardines with 1 tablespoon of butter, and then stir into the gravy, blending well, then add the drained capers (if you're fond of capers, use ½ cup), 1 tablespoon of chopped parsley, and the juice of half a lemon. When all is blended, add the meatballs to the gravy, reheat, and serve.

This will serve 4 to 6, depending upon the capacity of the diners. Boiled parsley potatoes, riced potatoes, or noodles go best with *Königsberger Klops*. Personally, I like cold mugs of beer best with this meal, but a good Rhine wine, chilled, is excellent. Coleslaw is a grand side dish.

Walter Trohan, chief of the Washington Bureau of the *Chicago Tribune*, is one of the Capitol's best-known correspondents as well as gourmets. He can whip up a delectable dish of his own devising almost as quickly as he can pound out a brilliant story on his typewriter, which is practically in nothing flat. Walter has created one of the most intriguing hamburger recipes I have ever come across.

HAMBURGERS WALTER TROHAN

1 *lb. ground round steak*   Salt
1 *small can of Smithfield*   Pepper

ham spread, or	Roquefort or blue cheese
deviled ham	Dry red wine
	Butter

Blend 1 small can Smithfield ham spread or deviled ham with 1 pound of fresh ground round steak. Add very little salt, and freshly ground pepper to taste.

Cut pieces of Roquefort or blue cheese into 1¼-inch squares, about ½ inch thick. Mold hamburgers around these squares, and put them in a crock. Cover the hamburgers with dry California red wine, and let them stand, covered, in the refrigerator for about 3 hours. At the end of the marinating time, put a little butter into a skillet, with a little of the marinade, and pan broil the hamburgers to taste (rare, medium, or well done). Remove them to a hot plate, add a little more butter and marinade to the pan, let boil up, and pour the sauce over the hamburgers.

Rib ends, or short ribs of beef, include a considerable amount of bone, but nevertheless they are most succulent. They are always braised or stewed.

Recently, however, I discovered a new way of cooking short ribs—broiling them, believe it or not, using Adolph's Instant Meat Tenderizer.

Today Adolph's Instant Meat Tenderizer is available in almost every part of the civilized world. And the company is finding new things the product will do. Lentils, split peas, lima and navy beans, soaked overnight in water to which a tablespoon of Adolph's has been added, cook in half the time. Soups and broths made from tenderized meat or fowl are tastier.

BROILED SHORT RIBS OF BEEF OONA LOA

3 lbs. lean beef short ribs	¼ cup soy sauce
1½ tsp. Adolph's Instant	1 tbsp. brown sugar
Seasoned Meat	¼ cup honey
Tenderizer	¼ cup water
1 cup pineapple juice	1½ tsp. ground ginger
	6 slices pineapple

Sprinkle the ribs evenly with the meat tenderizer and pierce generously from all sides with a kitchen fork or skewer.

Mix the pineapple juice, soy sauce, brown sugar, honey, water, and ground ginger together, and pour this sauce over the shortribs, and return the ribs to the refrigerator for 4 or 5 hours. When ready to cook, drain the meat, place on a broiler rack (or barbecue rack) about 3 inches from the flame or heat unit. Broil until the meat is well browned. Then turn, spoon well with the sauce, and broil until richly brown.

Five minutes before taking up the meat, brush the pineapple slices with the marinade sauce, and arrange on rack with meat. Let them heat through and brown slightly at the edges. These make a very pretty garnish for those shining brown ribs. Serves 6.

Roast lamb, to my mind, is a great delicacy, whether plain roasted or roasted with wine. But roast lamb with mint gravy is something superlative. Notice that I said mint *gravy,* not mint sauce.

I've always been very fond of mint in drinks and as a flavoring agent. But mint sauce has always been too thin to suit my taste. On the other hand, I like rich brown lamb gravy. So I said to myself, why can't they be combined? So, after a bit of experimentation, a mint gravy resulted. And for my money it is tops in the category of roast meat gravies.

ROAST LAMB PROVENÇAL WITH MINT GRAVY

1 6- to 7-lb. leg of lamb	Water
Garlic	Dry white wine
Flour	Bunch fresh mint
Salt	5 tablespoons sugar
Pepper	Cider vinegar
	Rosemary

In a 6- or 7-pound leg of lamb insert a number of slivers of garlic so that they are distributed throughout the meat. Then sprinkle the top of the leg of lamb with flour, salt and pepper, and rosemary. Put the lamb in a roaster, pour in 1 cup of dry California white wine and 1 cup of water, cover, and put in a 500-degree oven. Let it remain for a half hour, or until it begins to brown and a crust begins to form on top. Baste, turn the oven to 350 degrees, and let the lamb cook for 2 hours, basting it every half hour, and after each basting, squeezing a little lemon juice over it. At the end of 2 hours lift the leg of lamb out of the roaster, skim off the grease, and put the lamb back in and let cook for another half hour. If necessary during the cooking, add more white wine and water, in equal proportions.

The mint sauce should be made about 3 or 4 hours before the lamb has started cooking. Remove all the leaves and the tender tips of the stems from a bunch of fresh mint and chop them very fine. Put in a deep bowl, and add 5 rounded tablespoons of sugar. Cover this completely with cider vinegar. Stir well and cover. Let stand for about 6 hours, stirring every hour.

At the end of the 3-hour cooking time, remove the leg of lamb to a hot platter, and if the juices have concentrated too much, add a little more white wine. In the meantime make a flour-and-water paste. Put in a separate saucepan 3 tablespoons of flour and a couple of pinches of salt. Start mixing this well with dripping cold water. Keep whipping constantly as the water is added, until it has a creamy consistency.

Into the juices of the roasting pan stir the flour paste slowly, until the juices are thickened. The gravy should be thicker than the average gravy, as the mint sauce to be added will thin it out. When the gravy is perfectly smooth, add the mint sauce and again stir thoroughly. Serve this mint gravy in a separate gravy boat.

I can't conceive of finding lamb shanks on the menus of the Drake or Pump Room in Chicago, or the Savoy or the Colony Club in New York. But we prepare them at the Maison Wood, and if you prepare them the same way at your house, you'll agree that they rate orchids, raves, or four bells! I call them "Lamb Shanks Beatrice," with a deep bow to my wife, who concocted them.

LAMB SHANKS BEATRICE

4 *lamb shanks*	1 *cup chopped celery*
3 *slices of bacon*	½ *cup chopped parsley*
Flour	2 *medium-sized onions*
Salt	1 *clove garlic, chopped*
Pepper	1 *tsp. Worcestershire sauce*
1 *medium-sized can*	1 *tbsp. grated horseradish*
tomatoes	1 *cup dry red wine*

½ *lb. fresh mushrooms*

Render 3 slices of bacon, finely cut, then take out the bacon bits. Coat 4 lamb shanks thickly with seasoned flour, then brown them slowly in the bacon fat, turning on all sides until nicely browned. This should be done in a deep iron kettle, a Dutch oven, or a drip-drop roaster, without the top. When the shanks are browned, add a medium-sized can of tomatoes, the bacon bits, 1 cup of chopped celery, ½ cup of chopped parsley, 2 medium-sized onions, peeled and finely chopped, 1 finely chopped clove of garlic, 1 teaspoon of Worcestershire sauce, 1 tablespoon of grated horseradish, and 1 cup of dry California red wine (Burgundy type preferred). Cover this mixture and let it simmer for 2 hours. Then add ½ pound of fresh mushrooms, separating the stems from the tops and, if the mushrooms are very large, halving or quartering them. Now let the whole thing cook for about ½ to ¾ of an hour longer. If the gravy has not thickened to the desired stage, just before serving make a flour paste (flour and a little water) and thicken the gravy slightly. The gravy should not be watery, neither should it be very thick—just a nice consistency that allows you to get it all up with the crusty French bread that you should serve with this epicurean delight. Serves 4.

New potatoes, served with parsley butter, and new lima beans make a delicious accompaniment, and if you're really hungry, serve a tossed green salad, too. And, of course, serve dry red wine.

True Irish stew has mutton as its foundation, with, of course, potatoes and onions, and other vegetables on occasion, as ornaments. But mutton, in America, is far less tasty than the mutton one finds in the British Isles, so in this country lamb is used. And if you are of the opinion that a lamb stew can't be taste-tantalizing, just try this recipe.

LAMB STEW

2 lbs. lamb shoulder, cubed	1 tsp. salt
1 tsp. salt	¼ tsp. pepper
¼ cup flour	½ tsp. dried rosemary
3 tbsp. bacon drippings	2 cups potatoes, cubed
1 medium onion, sliced	1 cup snap beans
1 clove garlic, minced	1 cup diced carrots
1 cup light red wine	6-8 small white onions
4 cups boiling water	5 tbsp. flour
½ tsp. Ac'cent	5 tbsp. water

Get the shoulder of lamb cut in about 1-inch squares. Wipe with a damp cloth. Sprinkle with about 1 teaspoon of salt, and roll in flour.

In a heavy pot heat the bacon drippings, and then add the floured lamb cubes. Brown them well over a medium flame on all sides, then add the sliced onion and the minced garlic. When the onions are browned lightly, pour off all the fat from the pot and add to the pot the light dry red wine, the boiling water, the Ac'cent, the salt and pepper, and the dried rosemary. Cover the pot tightly, and simmer slowly until the meat is almost tender, about 1½ to 2 hours.

Next add to the pot the cubed potatoes, the green beans, cut as desired, the diced carrots, and the small white onions. Continue cooking until the vegetables and meat are tender, about 20 to 30 minutes.

Blend together the flour and water to form a smooth paste, and add this paste to the stew, stirring it in carefully so that no lumps will form. Then reheat the whole thing until it comes to a boil, and boil gently for half a minute. Then serve to 6.

Curry, or, as the Dutch call it, *rijstafel* (which means "rice table"), is the world's heavyweight champion food. It is a gastronomic miracle that rises to the pinnacle of perfection in the Dutch East Indies.

Let's say you are in the Batavia of the 1930's, seated at the table in the old Hotel Nederlanden, with a huge Dutch napkin tucked under your chin, and you order rice "toffel." Then things begin to happen!

Out of the kitchen comes a line of barefooted, gaily dressed waiters, each bearing a huge platter. The Number 1 boy offers a big bowl of snowy white rice, and you heap your plate with it. Then Number 2 boy offers another huge bowl, containing curry, usually made of chicken. You make a crater in your plateful of rice, and heap it to overflowing with the succulent, aromatic curry, spreading it evenly over the rice. And then the parade continues with Numbers 3, 4, 5, 6, and so on, boys.

Each boy carries a different delicacy. There are various kinds of chutney, vegetables, eggs, shrimps, fish, pickles, bananas, chopped nuts, raisins, coconut, pineapple, hors d'oeuvres, and what not. You help yourself to a portion of each, spreading it over the rice and curry, then you mix the entire outlay with your knife and fork. And then you proceed to eat, and I do mean eat!

Of course, in these days, it is questionable whether you have even one servant, or Number 1 boy, let alone anywhere from 11 to 22. But don't despair, because I'll tell you how to make a succulent curry and serve it, buffet style, all by yourself. It may look a touch difficult, but, believe me, it's not.

LAMB CURRY

2 *cooking apples*	1 *cup consommé*
1 *green pepper*	½ *cup dry red wine*
2 *onions*	1 *lemon, juice and grated*
1 *clove garlic (crushed)*	*rind*
2 *tbsp. olive oil*	½ *cup seedless raisins*
2 *tbsp. flour*	2 *whole cloves*

1 tbsp. curry powder	2 cups diced cold lamb
½ tsp. salt	(cooked)
½ tsp. marjoram	¼ cup shredded coconut
½ tsp. thyme	1 tbsp. sour cream

Core, pare, and slice 2 cooking apples, chop up a green pepper, and slice two peeled onions. Sauté these, together with a crushed clove of garlic, in 2 tablespoons olive (or cooking) oil, until onions are limp. Then sprinkle over the contents of the skillet 2 level tablespoons of flour, 1 level tablespoon of curry powder (the best), and ½ teaspoon each of salt, marjoram, and thyme. Mix the contents of the skillet well, stirring constantly, and cook for 5 minutes. Then add 1 cup of consommé, ½ cup of dry red wine, the juice of a lemon and its grated rind, ½ cup of seedless raisins, and 2 whole cloves. Let all this simmer for 20 to 30 minutes.

Now add 2 cups of diced cold cooked lamb (leave some of the fat on the lamb) and ¼ cup of shredded coconut. Let this heat for 15 minutes, and just before serving add a tablespoon of sour cream, mixing it well into the whole concoction.

On your buffet table have a large wooden bowl of hot, flaky rice. Next to it place your bowl of curry. And that's all there is to it. Of course, if you want to be swanky (and who doesn't?), you should have small dishes of condiments, with a small spoon in each, containing chutney, chopped sweet pickles, chopped hard-boiled eggs, chopped mild (or little green) onions, chopped nuts, shredded canned pineapple, and finely chopped orange peel. Turn the guests loose, telling them first to make a mound of rice on their plates, then cover it with curry, and finally to sprinkle a little of each condiment over the whole.

If it can be said that there is a traditional Easter dish in America, probably baked ham would be named. There are many ways of baking ham, all the way from using champagne down to ginger ale or cider. In rural Russia, fresh ham is even cooked with hay and beer. But I don't imagine that many people have ever had ham baked in crust with brandy. For most it will be a new gastronomic experience.

HAM BAKED IN CRUST WITH BRANDY

1 10-lb. tenderized ham	½ cup chopped herbs
1 cup brown sugar	(chives, parsley,
1 cup honey	tarragon, chervil, minced
2 tbsp. dry mustard	garlic, little
Whole cloves	green onion, oregano,
4 lb. rye flour	pinch nutmeg)
Beef bouillon	1 tsp. caraway seeds
	Brandy

Remove the skin and rind from a 10-pound tenderized ham. Score the surface of the remaining fat.

Make a thick paste of 1 cup of brown sugar, solidly packed, 1 cup of honey, and 2 tablespoons of dry mustard, thoroughly mixed. Smear this over the ham (the paste should be thick enough not to run down the side of the ham, but not too thick to spread evenly. If too thick, thin with a little brandy). Stick a number of cloves over the top of the ham, being generous with them.

Next make a pastry crust by mixing 4 pounds of rye flour with enough canned beef bouillon to make a thick dough. On a slightly floured breadboard, roll this dough out to about ½-inch thickness. Brush the dough with brandy, then sprinkle it with ½ cup of chopped mixed herbs, such as parsley, chervil, chives, tarragon, minced garlic, little green onion, oregano, and a pinch of nutmeg, all thoroughly mixed. Then scatter over the dough 1 teaspoon of caraway seeds. Now wrap the dough around the ham so it overlaps, forming a bottlelike opening on the top. Fashion a stopper of dough, roll it in flour, and set it lightly in the opening. Then put the encrusted ham in a 325-degree oven until the dough has set hard. Take the ham out, remove the stopper, and very slowly pour in all the brandy that the honey-sugar-mustard jacket will absorb. Then cork up the opening again, and bake in the same moderate oven for about 50 minutes more, or until the crust is thoroughly baked and brown. Break the crust and serve.

The usual method of cooking a ham steak is to broil, to pan broil it, or to bake it in milk, all of which methods are mighty good. But they can't hold a candle to a ham steak baked with port.

HAM STEAK BAKED WITH PORT

1 *slice of ham*	4 *tbsp. prepared mustard*
½ *cup brown sugar*	¾ *cup port wine*
	Watercress

Rub into both sides of a fairly thick slice of ham ½ cup of brown sugar. Then coat both sides with prepared mustard. About 4 tablespoons should be sufficient.

Place the prepared ham in a baking dish, and add ¾ cup of port wine. Bake in a moderate oven (350 degrees) for about 1 hour, basting occasionally with the port wine.

Remove the ham to a hot platter, skim off the fat, pour a little more port into the pan if necessary, stir well, and pour the sauce over the ham. Garnish with watercress.

One day a gourmet friend of mine, who is one of the chief editorial writers on the Chicago *Tribune*, called me on the phone and said, "Morry, you have a lot of succulent and high-grade recipes in your 'For Men Only!' columns, but how about a recipe for something that can be bought in a butcher shop where you'll have some change left out of a five-dollar bill—say, a pork roast?"

Well, I got busy dreaming up things that could be done to a pork roast, and I finally worked out a recipe that makes one of the most tantalizing dishes imaginable. And here it is.

HERBED PORK ROAST

1 4- to 5-lb. pork loin roast	Fennel (or anise) seed
Olive oil	Flour

Salt	1 cup chicken broth
Freshly ground pepper	½ cup sour cream
Dried thyme	¾ cup dry white wine
Dried oregano	1 clove garlic
Medium onion, thinly sliced	⅛ tsp. ground nutmeg
	2 tbsp. flour

2 tbsp. butter

Rub the pork loin roast lightly with the very best olive oil (I have tried a great many kinds, but years ago I settled on the Old Monk brand as the best I could find anywhere. It is made in Nice, France, and I have found that many of the leading restaurants in America use only the Old Monk Imported Olive Oil).

After annointing the meat with the olive oil, sprinkle it with salt, freshly ground pepper, dried thyme, dried oregano, the fennel (or anise) seeds, and flour. Lightly pat the roast, so that the herbs will adhere to it. Then fasten the onion slices, cut almost paper-thin, over all the meat with toothpicks. Wrap the prepared roast in Saran Wrap, and let it stand in the refrigerator for about 12 hours, so that the flavor of the herbs will be absorbed.

Just before putting the roast in the oven, make the basting liquor. Cook together in a saucepan for about 5 minutes the chicken broth (or canned chicken bouillon), the dry white wine, the minced clove of garlic, and grated nutmeg. Keep this warm.

To cook, remove the meat from the refrigerator, remove the wrapping, and place the meat in a roasting pan, rib side down. Place in a preheated 375-degree oven for 30 minutes. Then pour in the basting liquor, turn the oven down to 325 degrees, and let the roast cook for about 35 minutes to the pound (or, if a meat thermometer is used, roast until the thermometer registers 185 degrees for the inside of the roast), basting frequently.

To prepare the gravy, remove the roast to a hot platter and keep warm (leave the onion slices pinned on the roast; they will be almost black, but they have the most delicious flavor imaginable). Skim the excess fat from the basting liquor in the roaster, and add enough chicken broth and dry white wine (in equal parts) to make 2 cups of liquid. Have a *roux* prepared of 2 table-spoons each of flour and butter. Mix this *roux* with the liquid in the roaster (or add a little of the hot liquid to the *roux* and stir until it is a thin paste), and add the commercial sour cream. Cook, stirring constantly, until the gravy is thickened and smooth. Serve the gravy sep-arately.

One of my favorite pork dishes is pork tenderloin pat-ties, which was devised by my wife. We have it at home at least once a month, and both of us look forward to it. It is not too expensive, since there is no waste and it is easy to prepare. It is one of the top dishes on the pork parade, as far as I am concerned.

PORK TENDERLOIN PATTIES WITH WINE

1 *pork tenderloin, frenched*	½ *cup consommé*
into 6 patties	½ *cup dry white wine*
Seasoned flour	*Salt*
1 *tbsp. bacon drippings*	*Freshly ground pepper*
1 *tsp. flour*	*Celery salt*
½ *cup water*	*Garlic salt*
Dash Worcestershire sauce	

Have your butcher divide a pork tenderloin into 6 parts, and french them. Shake them in seasoned flour. Put the bacon drippings into a skillet, and when hot brown the tenderloin patties on both sides over a medium flame (if they show a tendency to stick, add a teaspoon or more of bacon drippings).

When the patties are nicely browned, sprinkle in and around the patties 1 heaping teaspoon of flour, and stir into the fat to make a *roux*. Then add the water, con-sommé, and dry white wine, salt and freshly ground pepper to taste, a sprinkle of celery salt and garlic salt, and a couple of dashes of Worcestershire sauce. Cover, and simmer over a low flame slowly for 45 minutes, stir-ring occasionally, and moving the patties in the gravy so they won't stick. This recipe will serve 3.

Cooking plain dishes is very simple, and not beyond the ability of almost any man, woman, or child above the age of twelve. Yet with a little imagination, or by following recipes whose directions are given in simple, orderly fashion, many gourmet dishes can be made from plain fare. For instance, let's take some plain fare—say pork chops—and make a gourmet dish.

PORK CHOPS IN SOUR CREAM AND MADEIRA

4 *loin pork chops*	⅓ *cup sour cream*
3 *tbsp. Madeira*	*Salt*
Pepper	

Pan broil 4 pork chops in the usual way. When tender, and a nice brown, remove them from the pan for a moment. If there is an excess of fat in the pan, pour it off. Then add 3 tablespoons of Madeira and ⅓ cup of sour cream, stirring well into the gravy, and scraping the pan to loosen any particles of meat that may adhere. Now return the pork chops to the pan, and cook for another five or ten minutes, frequently basting the chops.

One of the most celebrated examples of the French *cuisine bourgeois* comes from the province of Languedoc, in southern France. Its full name is *le Cassoulet de Midi*. Basically, it is a dish of French white beans cooked in a pot with various kinds of pork and sausage. But, depending on the region, other items are added. The original dish, from Castelnaudry, used ham, pork rind, fresh pork, and spiced sausages. In Carcassonne mutton and sometimes partridges are added. In Toulouse lamb and preserved goose also go into the pot.

The French white bean and preserved goose (*confit d'oie*) are rare in America. But in place of the French beans our navy beans, pinto beans, Italian white kidney beans, or "black-eyed Susans" can well be used. In place of the preserved goose, roast goose or roast duck may be used, although it is not essential. The following recipe combines the three Languedoc versions.

CASSOULET

2 lb. dried beans	6 peppercorns
½ lb. fresh pork rind, sliced.	1 bay leaf
¼ lb. bacon	1 lb. small pork sausages
2 onions	4 tbsp. lard
2 whole cloves	1 lb. boned shoulder pork
1 carrot	1 lb. boned breast lamb
6 cloves garlic	Salt
¼ tsp. dried thyme	Pepper
½ cup dry white wine	

Soak 2 pounds dried beans (of your choice) overnight in cold water. Drain beans and place in a pot or kettle together with ½ pound fresh pork rind slices tied in a bundle, ¼ pound bacon in 1 piece, 1 onion studded with 2 cloves, 1 carrot, 6 cloves garlic, minced, ¼ teaspoon dried thyme, 6 peppercorns, bruised, and a bay leaf. Cover contents completely with water (about 4 quarts) and bring to boil. Reduce flame and simmer very, very gently for about 1½ hours, or until beans are tender.

While beans are cooking lightly brown 1 pound small link sausages in a skillet. In another large skillet heat 4 tablespoons lard. Then add 1 medium onion, minced, and 1 pound each boned shoulder of pork and boned breast of lamb, both cut in ¾-inch cubes and seasoned with salt and pepper. Let cubes of meat brown on all sides, then pour in the skillet ½ cup dry white wine. Stir to loosen any meat particles. Let simmer for a couple of minutes, then add liquid in skillet to the beans, reserving cubes of meat.

When beans are cooked, remove onion and carrot and discard them. Also remove from beans the pork rind and bacon, and cut bacon into ½-inch cubes.

On the bottom of a large earthenware casserole place the pork rind in a layer, then add half of the beans. On top of bean layer place browned cubes of meat, the bacon cubes, and the sausages, each one cut in half. If you have any roast duck or goose left over, add it to the other meats. Then pour in the remaining beans and their juices. Cover casserole and put in a 225-degree oven, and let it cook at least 4 hours, or even longer, if you wish.

Serve to 6 or 8 from the casserole, giving a little of each meat and a generous portion of beans to each guest. I like crusty French bread and a dry white wine with this dish.

Not long ago I made barbecued spareribs, which I called Piquant Spareribs. The guests may not have enjoyed them, but it's the first time I ever saw sparks fly from knives and forks!

PIQUANT SPARERIBS

4 lbs. lean spareribs
1 cup mayonnaise
2 oz. dry sherry
2 oz. soy sauce
1 tsp. chili powder
1 tsp. powdered ginger
2 cloves garlic, minced
2 tbsp. Worcestershire sauce
1 tsp. hickory-smoked salt
2 tsp. horseradish

1 tsp. dry mustard
2 tbsp. tomato paste
½ tsp. black pepper
3 tbsp. brown sugar
6 oz. pineapple juice
1 tsp. onion juice
4 tsp. white wine tarragon vinegar
½ tsp. oregano
½ tsp. celery salt

Mix all the ingredients (except spareribs) until sauce is well blended. It will make a scant 3 cups.

Put the spareribs, cut into about 4-inch pieces, into a roaster, and place in a preheated 500-degree oven. Let them cook for about 30 minutes. Pour off the accumulated fat.

Cover the spareribs with about ⅓ of the sauce, and put in the oven, after reducing the heat to 300 degrees. After 30 minutes add the second third of the sauce, and cook for another 30 minutes. Then add the balance of the sauce, and cook for another 30 minutes, or until the spareribs are tender.

Remove the spareribs to a hot platter, skim off any fat that has accumulated, and then pour the sauce over the spareribs, and serve. This will serve 4 people generously.

If ribs are barebecued, do not cut them in pieces. Brush them liberally and frequently with the sauce while cooking. The sauce may be kept warm while the ribs are cooking, and any remaining sauce may be poured over the spareribs.

I think my favorite veal dish is Veal Scallopini Marsala. I am not an Italian, and yet I have never found Veal Scallopini Marsala in any Italian restaurant, even the finest, that even approached my recipe. But you, dear reader, can make it just as well as I can if you will heed my warning as to some of the ingredients. First, use only the best olive oil; second, use only imported Parmesan or Romano cheese, and third, use only the imported Florio Marsala, because it is virgin dry while most of the others are too sweet. The dish is really simple to prepare and cook—here's the recipe.

VEAL SCALLOPINI MARSALA

1 *lb. veal cutlet*	1 *clove garlic*
½ *cup grated Parmesan cheese*	½ *cup consommé*
	2 *tsp. lemon juice*
Salt	*Marjoram*
Pepper	*Thyme*
2 *tbsp. olive oil*	½ *cup Florio Marsala*

Get a veal cutlet weighing about 1 pound, and cut not more than 1 inch thick. Place it on a wooden board, sprinkle it generously with grated Parmesan cheese, and pound it with a wooden mallet or wooden potato masher. Then turn it over, sprinkle again generously with the grated Parmesan cheese, and pound it again. Repeat this process until you have used about ½ cup of the grated cheese and the cutlet has become between ¼ and ½ inch thick. Sprinkle on both sides with salt and pepper, then cut the meat into 3-inch strips, each about 1 inch wide.

Heat 2 tablespoons olive oil with a crushed clove of garlic in it, and then put in the meat and brown it on both sides. Add ½ cup of consommé, ½ cup of Florio

Marsala, and 2 teaspoons of lemon juice. As this begins
to cook, add a pinch each of marjoram and thyme. Then
cover the skillet and simmer slowly for about 30 minutes,
or until the veal is tender.

Here's another veal dish that will sharpen the most
dulled appetite and start the nostrils quivering.

VEAL CHOPS PARMESAN IN WHITE WINE

4 *veal chops*	*Flour*
Lime juice	*Grated Parmesan cheese*
Salt	*1 beaten egg*
Freshly ground pepper	*2 tbsp. butter*
¾ *cup dry white wine*	

Trim 4 veal chops, brush with lime juice, sprinkle with
salt and freshly ground pepper, then dip them first in hot
butter, then in flour, and then in grated Parmesan cheese.
Let them remain thus until they are well soaked. Then dip
them in the beaten egg, once more in flour, and then in
the grated cheese, and let the seasoning soak in for about
2 hours.

When ready to cook sauté the chops quickly in 2 tablespoons of hot butter until they are browned on both
sides. Then pour into the skillet around the chops ¾ cup
of dry American white wine. Cover, and simmer slowly
for 30 to 40 minutes, or until very tender.

Boiled macaroni, well buttered and sprinkled with
grated Parmesan cheese, is practically a "must" with this
delectable dish.

One of the most famous and delicious dishes in the
realm of gastronomy is *Wiener Schnitzel.* The true
Wiener Schnitzel, prepared in the traditional style of old,
prewar Vienna at such restaurants as Sacher's or the
Hotel Bristol, is a delicate morsel that will set your taste
buds tingling with delight. And it is very simple to prepare, too.

WIENER SCHNITZEL

2 lb. young veal	2 eggs
Lemon juice	2 tbsp. dry white wine
½ lb. butter	1 cup fine bread crumbs
Salt	¼ cup flour
Freshly ground pepper	12 anchovy fillets
Pinch paprika	

Have the veal cut from the leg in slices ¼ inch thick. Trim, and cut the cutlets into individual serving pieces. Place the pieces between several thicknesses of waxed paper, and pound gently with a flat-faced wooden mallet, or the flat side of a cleaver, until the pieces are ⅛ inch thick. Then marinate the pieces for 1 hour in enough lemon juice to cover the meat. Then remove them from the lemon juice, dry, and sprinkle both sides with salt and freshly ground pepper.

Beat 2 whole eggs lightly in a bowl with the dry white wine. Draw each of the veal pieces through the beaten egg, first on one side then on the other. Dredge the pieces with fine bread crumbs mixed with the flour, and gently pat the coating in. Allow to stand for 15 to 20 minutes.

Melt the butter in a large skillet and let it foam well. Reduce the flame and sauté the cutlets for 1½ minutes on each side. The cutlets are done when the coating turns to a golden brown. Drain the sautéed cutlets on paper toweling, then place on a very hot platter.

To the butter in the skillet (add more if necessary) add the 12 mashed anchovy fillets and a generous pinch of paprika. When blended, pour over the cutlets, first having sprinkled them lightly with lemon juice. Serve immediately. Buttered noodles are almost a must with *Wiener Schnitzel*.

The classic veal dish in France is *Blanquette de Veau*. It is a ragout, or stew, of veal with a white sauce, and properly prepared it is a gastronomic masterpiece without peer. It is also an economical dish, and while it takes a little time to prepare, it is quite easy.

BLANQUETTE DE VEAU
(Veal Stew)

2 lb. lean veal
1 qt. water
1 tsp. salt
1 large onion
2 whole cloves
2 small carrots
Pinch dried thyme
½ cup celery leaves
1 clove garlic
1 tbsp. chopped parsley
1 bay leaf
5 peppercorns

7 tbsp. butter
12 small white onions
½ lb. fresh mushrooms
Salt
Pepper
2 tbsp. flour
2 cups veal broth
½ cup dry white wine
2 oz. French (dry)
    vermouth
2 egg yolks
1 cup cream

1 tsp. lemon juice

Get 2 pounds of lean veal, and cut the meat into cubes about 1 to 1½ inches. Bring 1 quart of water to a boil in a deep saucepan after adding a teaspoon of salt. Add the cubes of veal slowly, so the water continues to boil. Then add 1 large peeled onion cut in half, and each half stuck with a whole clove, 2 small carrots, sliced, a pinch dried thyme, a handful of celery leaves, a minced clove garlic, 1 tablespoon of chopped parsley, a bay leaf, and 5 whole peppercorns. Cover the saucepan, turn down the flame, and simmer until veal is tender, about 1½ hours.

While veal is cooking melt 3 tablespoons of butter in a heavy saucepan and add 12 small peeled white onions. Cook until lightly browned, then lower flame and steam until they are tender, about 30 minutes. Also sauté ½ pound of mushrooms, sliced, in 2 tablespoons butter until tender, about 6 minutes, and season with salt and pepper to taste.

When veal is tender remove pieces to a serving casserole, and add to veal pieces the small onions and mushrooms, and keep all warm. Then strain the broth, discarding the solids.

In a deep saucepan or skillet melt 2 tablespoons of butter and blend in 2 tablespoons of flour. Do not, however, let the flour brown. When *roux* is well blended, slowly add 2 cups of the strained broth, ½ cup of dry white wine, and 2 ounces of dry (French) vermouth. Stir constantly while liquid is being added until smooth and slightly thickened. Bring just to the boiling point, then lower flame to a simmer. Add to the sauce 2 beaten egg yolks mixed with 1 cup of cream, stirring constantly. Cook very gently (do not allow to boil) until sauce is smooth and thickened. Correct seasoning, if necessary, and add 1 teaspoon of lemon juice.

To the sauce add the veal cubes, small onions, and mushrooms, reheat gently, and return all to the warm serving casserole. Sprinkle over all a generous tablespoon chopped fresh parsley, and serve. With this dish serve fluffy cooked rice, buttered peas, and, of course, a chilled dry white wine. Serves 5.

I am going to start with an assertion that will be difficult to contradict: Either you like kidneys or you don't. Now, I am going to make a suggestion: If you don't like them, forget your inhibitions and try the following receipe for ragout of kidney.

LAMB KIDNEY STEW WITH WINES AND BRANDY

12 *lamb kidneys*	*Salt*
1 *lb. mushrooms*	*Pepper*
6 *little green onions*	½ *cup dry white wine*
¼ *green pepper*	2 *ounces Madeira*
4 *tbsp. butter*	2 *ounces brandy*
1 *tbsp. chopped parsley*	½ *cup sour cream*

Wash 12 lamb kidneys in cold water, remove the outer skin, and soak them in salted water for 2 or 3 hours. Then cut them in half, remove the white centers and tubes with a sharp pointed knife, and slice them thin.

Slice 1 pound of fresh mushrooms. Chop 6 little green onions very fine and chop ¼ green pepper, after removing the seeds. That's your preliminary work.

Sauté the chopped onions and the chopped green peppers in 4 tablespoons of butter slowly until they are slightly browned. Then add the sliced kidneys, the pound of sliced mushrooms, 1 tablespoon of chopped parsley, salt and freshly ground pepper to taste, ½ cup of dry American white wine, 2 ounces of Madeira, and 2 ounces of brandy. Cover and simmer gently for about 1½ hours, stirring every once in a while. Shortly before serving add ½ cup of sour cream. Cook a few minutes longer, check for seasoning, and serve.

Liver and bacon and liver and onions are probably the two best-known liver dishes, but on too many cook stoves they are horribly mistreated. When liver has been cooked too slowly and too long, especially when fried, it is frequently tough and flavorless. When perfectly cooked, its juices are pinkish, its flavor is superb, and it is as tender as a woman's heart. . . . Well, anyway, tender.

The Italians have a marvelous way of cooking liver and onions, as follows:

LIVER AND ONIONS, ITALIAN STYLE

8 *thin liver slices*	*Flour*
½ *cup dry red wine*	*Salt*
4 *medium-sized onions*	*Pepper*
6 *tbsp. olive oil*	1 *pinch oregano*

Add about ½ cup of California dry red wine to 8 thin liver slices, and let stand in the refrigerator for an hour or so, turning the liver occasionally. About ½ hour before serving time sauté 4 sliced medium-sized onions in about 4 tablespoons of olive oil until lightly browned. Then remove them and keep them hot. Add about 2 more tablespoons of olive oil to the skillet, drain the liver slices, keeping the marinade, roll in seasoned flour, and brown them, adding a little more butter or oil if needed. The cooking time should be about 3 or 4 minutes to each side. Take out the liver and keep it hot. To the fat in the skillet add 1 tablespoon of flour and a pinch of oregano, blend well, and then stir in the wine in which the liver was marinated. Cook, stirring, until the gravy is smooth and slightly thickened. Season to taste. Arrange the liver and onions on a hot platter, and pour the wine gravy over all.

Tongue, either smoked or fresh, may be prepared in a number of ways. Of course, the simplest is to boil it in water until tender, with herbs and spices added to the water, and then serve it with some sort of sauce (my favorite is a creamed horseradish sauce). Tongue also may be baked, grilled, or braised. A very delectable, yet inexpensive, tongue dish is called Spiced Tongue with Burgundy.

SPICED TONGUE WITH BURGUNDY

1 2- to 3-lb. veal tongue	2 bay leaves
Boiling water	1 medium onion, minced
Salt	2 carrots, sliced
2 cups dry red wine	½ cup celery, chopped
2 cups tongue broth	1 cup raisins
½ tsp. allspice	Flour
12 whole cloves	Lemon slices
	Watercress

Scrub the veal tongue well, place in a kettle, and cover with boiling water to which a small amount of salt has been added. Cook about 2 hours. Then remove the tongue, peel off the skin, and remove the root ends.

In a deep iron pot heat the dry red wine and the tongue broth. Add the allspice, the cloves, bay leaves, the minced onion, the sliced carrots, the chopped celery, and the raisins. Place the tongue in this, and cook for an hour longer.

Remove the tongue and cut it in thin slices and arrange them on a hot platter. Thicken the sauce with a little flour and water paste, heat, and then pour over the slices of tongue. Garnish the platter with watercress and lemon slices.

Tripe is a favorite dish in most of the countries of

Europe, but in France it can be listed as almost indispensable. One of the great restaurants in Paris, Pharamond's, was made famous by a dish that originated in the medieval city of Caen, better known for its stone quarries. At Pharamond's, *Tripe à la Mode de Caen* is served in individual pewter plates, with small ovens built into them in which glowing charcoal is placed to keep the heavenly dish bubbling hot as one eats it.

TRIPE À LA MODE DE CAEN

3 *lb. fresh honeycomb tripe*	*Thyme*
4 *slices fat salt pork*	*Marjoram*
2 *sliced carrots*	*Mace*
2 *sliced onions*	2 *large bay leaves*
2 *chopped tomatoes*	8 *small peppercorns*
2 *leeks*	2 *whole cloves*
2 *stalks celery*	1 *teaspoon salt*
1 *large green pepper*	*Cayenne pepper*
1 *clove garlic*	1 *cup bouillon*
2 *calf's feet (meat and*	1 *cup dry white wine*
bones)	6 *little green onions*
1 *tbsp. minced parsley*	1 *cup brandy*

Wash 3 pounds of fresh honeycomb tripe in two or three changes of cold water, drain, and cut in strips about ¾ inch wide and 2½ to 3 inches long. Line the bottom of an earthenware casserole (or a metal Dutch oven) with 4 slices of fat salt pork. Add 2 sliced carrots, 2 sliced onions, 2 chopped tomatoes, 2 leeks, 2 stalks of celery, 1 large green pepper rather finely minced, and a clove of garlic, also minced. Over this vegetable layer arrange the strips of tripe, and add 2 calf's feet (meat and bones) cut up.

Season with 1 tablespoon of minced parsley, a generous pinch each of thyme, marjoram, and mace, 2 large bay leaves, 8 small peppercorns, slightly bruised, 2 whole cloves, 1 teaspoon salt, and a slight sprinkling of cayenne pepper. Cover the whole with equal parts of beef bouillon and dry California white wine—probably a cup of each will be sufficient. Now, put the cover on the pot, seal with flour and water paste, and bake in the slowest possible oven overnight, or for at least 12 hours.

When you break the seal and remove the cover, your nostrils will be assailed by the most heavenly odor you have ever experienced. But a final step remains. Add 6 finely minced little green onions and a cup of brandy. Heat again, and serve bubbling hot.

7· GAME

It frequently has been said that the cooking of game belongs entirely in male hands; that the Little Woman who normally presides in the kitchen hasn't (a) culinary imagination, (b) learned the art of cooking improvisation, or (c) had any experience to speak of with game cookery.

Although it may be *lèse majesté,* I am going to disagree for two reasons. The first is that I am thoroughly in accord with the Duc de Talleyrand, who said, "There are two things essential to life: to give good dinners and to keep on fair terms with women." The second reason is that a recipe for one of the most delicious duck dishes I ever ate came from a woman.

Ducks were highly prized as a delicacy by the Greeks and Romans in the days of antiquity. In the Middle Ages ducks were hunted with a bow and arrow (a feat I'd give a pretty penny to see some of my duck-hunting friends perform today). But I venture to say that even in the dim past, arguments went on as to the proper length of time to cook a duck. On this question I am a middle-of-the-roader. Let those who like wild ducks cooked 6 minutes cook them 6 minutes, but don't tender me an invitation to partake of them. And let those who like them overcooked (and tough) overcook them. I'll duck that invitation, too.

Probably the most conventional way to cook wild duck is to roast it, either with or without stuffing. Young mallards and canvasbacks are said to be at the peak of succulence broiled. But my favorite recipe is Duck à la Frederic, as prepared by my old friend, the late Ric Riccardo.

DUCK À LA FREDERIC RICCARDO

4 *mallards*	4 *tbsp. currant jelly*
2 *large carrots*	1 *tbsp. Worcestershire sauce*
2 *large onions*	*Juice from 2 pressed duck*
¼ *lb. butter*	*carcasses*
1 *clove garlic*	*Salt*
Rind 1 *orange*	*Pepper*
1 *tbsp. chopped parsley*	4 *ounces Marsala*

Stuff each of 4 mallards (or canvasbacks) with ½ of a large carrot and ½ of a large peeled onion. Place in a roasting pan and bake in a 400-degree oven for exactly 12 minutes. Then carve out the breasts from the ducks, remove the skin, and set them aside. Take the remaining carcasses of two of the ducks, place them in a duck press and extract the essences, and reserve for a moment. In a large skillet melt ¼ pound of butter, to which a mashed clove of garlic has been added. When the butter is bubbling, put the duck breasts in, and sauté them for one minute on each side. Remove the breasts to a warm platter, remove the clove of garlic from the butter, and add to the butter in the skillet the juices from the pressed ducks, the finely chopped rind of an orange, 1 tablespoon of chopped parsley, 4 tablespoons of currant jelly, 1 tablespoon of Worcestershire sauce, salt and pepper to taste, and 4 ounces of Marsala. Blend this well, then return the breasts to the sauce, and sauté the breasts for 30 seconds more on each side. Then place the breasts on a hot platter, pour the sauces over them, and serve with wild rice, bananas fried in bread crumbs, a tossed green salad, and a good Burgundy.

For some reason oranges seem to go with ducks just as ham goes with eggs. One of the outstanding recipes for duck goes back, I am told, to a fifteenth-century

Italian cook book. It is called Duck à la Jus Orange, and to me there is no duck recipe that tops it.

DUCK À LA JUS ORANGE

Pair of wild ducks	*1½ tbsp. minced celery tops*
Orange juice	*1½ tbsp. minced sweet basil*
Brandy	*1 tsp. gin*
1 cup uncooked wild rice	*Salt*
Boiling water	*Freshly ground pepper*
1 cup boiling chicken broth	*Duck giblets*
4 tbsp. sweet butter	*1 tsp. grated orange rind*
1½ tbsp. minced chives	*2 tsp. lemon juice*
1½ tbsp. minced parsley	*2 cups dry red wine*
1½ tbsp. minced little green	*3 tbsp. curaçao*
onions	*Tiny pinch nutmeg*

Rub a pair of wild ducks, which have been drawn and cleaned, with an equal portion of orange juice and brandy, inside and out.

Wash 1 cup of wild rice. Put 4 cups of boiling water, to which 1 teaspoon of salt has been added, in the top of a double boiler directly over the fire, and add the rice slowly without checking the boiling, and cook for 5 minutes. Then place it over boiling water in the under part of the double boiler, add 1 cup of boiling chicken broth, cover tightly, and steam from 30 to 45 minutes, or until the rice is tender.

While the rice is steaming, cream 4 tablespoons of sweet butter, brought to room temperature, with 1½ tablespoons each of finely minced chives, parsley, little green onions, green celery tops, and sweet basil. Then season this butter with 1 teaspoon of gin, salt and freshly ground pepper to taste, and a tiny pinch of freshly grated nutmeg.

Put the prepared butter in a saucepan, melt, and add the wild rice and the chopped giblets of the ducks. Cook briefly, tossing the rice until it is thoroughly impregnated with the prepared butter. Then stuff the ducks with the rice and giblets.

Put the ducks in an open roasting pan, and pour into

the pan 1 cup of orange juice, 1 teaspoon of grated orange rind, 2 teaspoons of lemon juice, and 1 cup of dry California red wine. Place the roaster in a 400-degree oven, and roast from 15 to 25 minutes, depending on the size and age of birds, basting frequently. Remove the ducks to a very hot platter.

Add another ¾ to 1 cup of red wine to the juices in the roaster, scraping the pan well to dislodge any particles of duck, and also add 3 tablespoons of curaçao. Bring to a boil on top of the stove; pour the sauce over the ducks, and serve.

Baring my breast to the slings and arrows of possibly outraged duck authorities throughout this fair land, I make bold to give my recipe for a roast wild duck. It ain't raw, it ain't burned to a crisp, and it ain't bad! As a matter of fact, my wife and I have found it damn good, and so have duck-loving guests who have savored it.

WOOD'S ROAST WILD DUCK

1 *wild duck* (1½ *lbs.*)	*Pepper*
1 *small apple*	*Brandy*
1 *small onion*	1 *cup orange juice*
1 *small stalk celery*	1 *cup dry red wine*
1 *slice bacon*	1½ *tbsp. orange curaçao*
2 *slices orange*	3 *tbsp. sour cream*
Salt	*Butter*

Rub the well-cleaned duck inside and out with a brandy-soaked cloth. Then sprinkle with salt and pepper inside and out.

Cut a small peeled and cored apple in quarters, and insert it, together with a small onion and a small stalk of celery, in the duck's cavity. Truss the duck, and rub the breast with soft butter. Lay the duck in a roasting pan, and place two half slices of bacon across the breast, and top the bacon slices with 2 thin orange slices.

Put the duck into a preheated 450-degree oven for about 8 minutes. Then pour in ½ cup each of orange juice and dry red wine in the roaster, and reduce the oven heat to 375 degrees. Baste the duck from time to time. After about 30 minutes of roasting, the liquid in the roaster will be almost dried up, and at that point add another ½ cup each of orange juice and dry red wine. Continue to roast the duck for about an hour from the time the oven heat was reduced.

Remove the duck to a hot platter and keep warm while making the gravy. Place the roaster on top of the stove, over a medium flame, and scrape the bottom to dislodge any particles of duck that might adhere. To the liquid in the pan add 1½ tablespoons of orange curaçao and 3 tablespoons of sour cream. Blend well until the gravy is smooth, then pour into a gravy boat. Serves 2.

BRANDIED WILD DUCK

Pair of wild ducks	*½ tsp. thyme*
Salt	*½ tsp. marjoram*
Pepper	*¼ tsp. allspice*
4 oz. brandy	*1 bay leaf*
1 cup dry red wine	*1 tbsp. butter*
2 large onions	*3 oz. olive oil*
1 tbsp. chopped parsley	*1 clove garlic*
	½ lb. fresh mushrooms

Disjoint a pair of wild ducks, and place the pieces in an earthenware or enamel crock or in a large bowl. Sprinkle them with salt and pepper and add 4 ounces of brandy, 1 cup of dry California red wine, 2 large onions, peeled and chopped, 1 tablespoon of chopped parsley, ½ teaspoon each of thyme and marjoram, ¼ teaspoon of allspice, and 1 bay leaf. Allow this to stand about 5 hours at room temperature, turning the pieces of duck occasionally.

In a heavy skillet or Dutch oven put 1 tablespoon of butter, 3 ounces of pure olive oil, and 1 crushed clove of garlic. When hot, add the pieces of duck, and brown well on all sides, about 15 or 20 minutes. Then add ½ pound of fresh mushrooms, sliced, and the strained mari-

nade. Cover, and simmer until the duck is tender—
about 1½ hours.

Serve from the casserole; or remove the duck to a hot
platter, thicken the sauce slightly by vigorous boiling,
and pour the sauce over the duck.

Of all game birds, pheasant is my favorite. To me it
has a succulency and perfume that no other bird pos-
sesses. Properly cooked, its flesh is tender, sublime, and
tastes of chicken and venison. As a matter of fact,
pheasant can be cooked in nearly all the ways that
chicken can be cooked—broiled, roasted, baked, stewed,
or sautéed. One of the easiest and most delicious ways of
cooking pheasant is what I call smothering.

SMOTHERED PHEASANT

1 *pheasant*	*Marjoram*
4 *small onions*	*½ cup consommé*
5 *stalks celery*	*½ cup dry red wine*
Butter	*Chopped parsley*
Flour	*Salt*
Thyme	*Pepper*

Disjoint the cleaned and plucked pheasant, shake the
pieces in a bag containing seasoned flour until they are
thoroughly coated, then lay them in a roaster or a Dutch
oven. Around them place four peeled onions (as many
as six can be used, depending on size). Sprinkle the
pieces with a generous pinch each of thyme, marjoram,
and chopped parsley. Liberally dot the pieces of pheasant with pieces of butter the size of grapes. Lay 5 single
stalks of celery, leaves and all, across the pheasant pieces
and the onions. Next, pour into the roaster ½ cup each
of consommé and dry California red wine. Cover, and
place in a hot oven (450-500 degrees) for about ½
hour, basting once. Then turn down the oven to 300 degrees, and cook for about 1½ hours, adding more wine,
as necessary, and basting at least every half hour. Next,
uncover, turn up the oven for a quick browning, and
then remove the pheasant, onions, and celery to a hot
platter. Put the roaster on top of the stove over a medium
flame, add a little more red wine, scraping the pan well

to loosen any particles of the dish that adhere, and when the gravy is heated, pour over the pheasant, onions, and celery.

Some gourmets prefer their pheasant roasted without any stuffing, or with just an onion or a bit of celery inside the bird. But I don't think any epicure would turn up his nose at a roast pheasant with brandied orange stuffing.

ROAST PHEASANT WITH BRANDIED ORANGE STUFFING

2 *cock pheasants*	*Salt*
3 *cups bread crumbs*	*Pepper*
3 *oz. butter*	2 *cups diced celery*
3 *oz. brandy*	*Pinch chervil*
2 *tbsp. grated orange rind*	*Pinch marjoram*
⅔ *cup orange pulp*	*Pinch rosemary*
1 *egg*	1 *cup dry red wine*

This recipe calls for 2 fat cock pheasants, ready for cooking.

For the stuffing, sauté 3 cups of bread crumbs in 1 ounce of butter. Mix with these 3 ounces of brandy, 2 tablespoons of grated orange peel, ⅔ cup of orange pulp, 2 cups of diced celery, 2 ounces of melted butter, 1 beaten egg, salt and pepper to taste, and a pinch each of chervil, marjoram, and rosemary. When all is thoroughly mixed, stuff the pheasants with the mixture, truss them, and place in an uncovered roaster. Add 1 cup of dry California red wine, and place the roaster in a moderate oven (350 degrees). Roast for 30 minutes per pound per bird, basting frequently with the red wine. If necessary, add more red wine during the roasting period.

When the birds are tender, remove to a hot platter, pour the pan juices over them, and serve.

I thought of calling the following recipe Roast Goose United Nations, but as some individuals are "agin" that world organization, I shall call it Roast Goose International. There's a hint of many countries among the ingredients, even Iraq.

ROAST GOOSE INTERNATIONAL

1 10- to 12-lb. goose	2 medium onions
Applejack	½ cup chopped celery
Salt	1 bay leaf
Pepper	¼ tsp. fennel seeds
3 cups rye-bread crumbs	¼ tsp. ground nutmeg
½ lb. dried prunes	¼ tsp. dried tarragon
Dry white wine	1 tbsp. chopped parsley
3 tbsp. butter	¼ lb. diced cooked ham
1 tsp. lemon juice	⅓ cup ground almonds
3 pears	Powdered ginger
3 apples	1 tbsp. currant jelly

Clean and singe a 10- to 12-pound young goose, and rub it inside and out with applejack which has been seasoned with salt and pepper.

Crumble 6 to 8 slices of rye-bread with caraway seeds in it, or enough to make 3 cups of bread crumbs.

Soak ½ pound of prunes in water overnight, then cook until tender in enough dry white wine to cover. When the prunes are cool, pit them and reserve, also reserving the wine they were cooked in.

In a large skillet melt the butter, and when it is hot, add the lemon juice, the chopped apples, pears, onions, and celery. Sauté this for about 6 minutes. Then add the crumbled bay leaf, fennel seeds, ground nutmeg, dried tarragon, chopped parsley, salt and pepper to taste, and a total of 1 cup of applejack (utilize any of the seasoned applejack that remains after anointing the goose). Cook until the apples and pears are tender, stirring the whole occasionally. Then put the contents of the skillet through a fine sieve, rubbing the solids through, into a large bowl.

To the contents of the bowl, add the bread crumbs, diced cooked ham, the ground almonds, and the cooked prunes. Mix everything well. If the stuffing seems too dry, moisten with applejack. The stuffing should be fluffy, not too moist. Stuff the goose with it.

Sew up or skewer the vent, truss the goose, and brush

it with melted butter seasoned with a little powdered ginger. Prick the skin in several places to allow the fat to run out. Place the goose in a covered roaster, breast side down, and roast in a 400-degree oven for 1 hour. Drain off all the grease, and add the wine the prunes were cooked in (and enough more, if necessary, to make 1 cup) and 1 cup of water. Place the goose breast side up, and cook until done, about 3 hours (allow 20 minutes to the pound total roasting time), basting frequently.

When goose is done, remove to a hot platter. Skim off any fat, and measure remaining liquid. If necessary, add enough dry wine to make 3 cups. Add a tablespoon each of applejack and currant jelly. Blend in enough flour-and-butter *roux* to make the gravy a good consistency. Heat, and serve in a gravy boat.

One of the tastiest breakfast dishes I know of is to take a partridge, salt and pepper it, and broil it, basting with plenty of butter. But for a regal dinner dish, I would like to recommend Partridges *à la Chasseur*.

PARTRIDGES À LA CHASSEUR

3 *partridges*	1 *tbsp. chopped parsley*
Salt	Generous pinch thyme
Pepper	Generous pinch marjoram
2 *tbsp. butter*	2 *tbsp. flour*
2 *oz. brandy*	1 *cup consommé*
4 *little green onions*	½ *cup dry white wine*
1 *carrot*	2 *cups fresh mushrooms*

Disjoint 3 partridges as you would young chickens, and rub the pieces well with salt and pepper.

In a skillet melt 2 tablespoons of butter. When hot, put the pieces of partridges in and brown them on both sides—about 15 minutes. Then pour over the partridges 2 ounces of brandy, and set alight. When the flame dies out, add to the pan 4 little green onions, chopped fine, 1 carrot, chopped fine, 1 tablespoon chopped parsley, and a generous pinch each of thyme and marjoram. Let these ingredients brown for about 2 or 3 minutes, and then sprinkle in 2 tablespoons of flour. Blend well, and then stir in 1 cup of consommé, ½ cup of dry California white wine, and 2 cups of sliced fresh mushrooms. Salt and pepper to taste. Simmer, covered, for about 25 to 30 minutes, or until the partridges are tender.

Serve partridges and sauce, using croutons as a garnish.

Regardless of whether they are fish, fowl, or game, in my opinion, frogs' legs—*Jambes des Grenouille*, as the French call them—make one of the most delicious and delicate morsels in the world. You will be able to get Frogs' Legs à la Provençal cooked to the queen's taste throughout France, even in the humblest inn, and you can prepare them in your own home with a minimum of fuss and effort so that they will be just as delicious as in France.

FROGS' LEGS PROVENÇAL

12 *medium-sized frogs' legs*	*Pepper*
5 *tbsp. butter*	2 *tbsp. tarragon*
2 *cloves garlic, crushed*	2 *tbsp. chopped chives*
Juice ½ lemon	2 *tbsp. chopped parsley*
Salt	1 *oz. brandy*
2 *oz. dry white wine*	

Wash the frogs' legs well in lemon juice and water, dry, and dust with flour. (The number you need depends on their size. I avoid very small ones or very large ones. There is not enough meat on the former, and the latter are likely to be a little tough. The recipe here calls for about a dozen medium-sized legs.) Put about 5 tablespoons of butter in a pan or skillet, heat to a point where it foams, and add 2 cloves of garlic, crushed, and the juice of ½ lemon.

Cook this for 1 minute, and then put in the frogs' legs. Shake them in the pan until they are golden brown on each side, then add salt and pepper to taste and 2 tablespoons each of finely chopped tarragon, chives, and parsley (the latter two should be fresh, the tarragon can be dried). Cook for another minute, and then add

1 ounce of lighted brandy and 2 ounces of good California white wine. Let cook for another minute, then rush the result to the table in a very hot dish.

Gastronomically speaking, rabbit is one of the most versatile of edible animals. The tender, delicately flavored meat of domestic rabbits (which are dressed with the same care afforded chickens) takes wonderfully to a variety of sauces and seasonings and methods of cooking. The wild rabbit is most plentiful; it may be cooked in any of the ways suitable for the domestic rabbit. Furthermore, rabbit is inexpensive and may be used in as many ways as poultry, and in the same ways.

One of the classic British dishes is jugged hare.

JUGGED HARE

1 *young rabbit, disjointed*	4 *slices bacon*
4 *tbsp. brandy*	1 *lemon rind, grated*
4 *tbsp. olive oil*	3 *tbsp. chopped parsley*
Salt	1 *tsp. dried thyme*
Freshly ground pepper	2 *bay leaves, minced*
1 *onion, sliced*	*Pinch powdered cloves*
2 *bay leaves*	8 *small onions*
Pinch dried thyme	1 *tbsp. mushroom catsup*
1 *clove garlic*	*Beef bouillon*
3 *whole cloves*	*Liver of rabbit*
Dry red wine	1 *tbsp. butter*
Flour	½ *cup port wine*

1 *tbsp. currant jelly*

Have your rabbit or hare cut into serving pieces by cutting the back into 2 pieces, and severing every joint. And be sure to get out the liver, which should be freed from the gall bladder and those portions touching it, washed, and reserved.

(If any of the male members of the family have gone out on a rabbit hunt, and returned with a young, plump wild rabbit or hare, it should be skinned and cleaned thoroughly, the blood collected, and the rabbit disjointed as directed above. The blood is used in making the sauce, which adds to its flavor. But if you are using a domestic rabbit, the blood is not necessary.)

Place the rabbit pieces in a crock, and add the brandy, olive oil, salt and freshly ground pepper to taste, the sliced onion, the bay leaves, dried thyme, the crushed clove of garlic, the cloves, and enough dry red wine to cover. Mix everything well, cover the crock, and let the rabbit pieces marinate for about 6 hours.

Remove the rabbit pieces from the crock, drain, and flour. In the bottom of a casserole lay the bacon slices, then put in a layer of rabbit pieces. Sprinkle with a mixture of seasonings (the grated lemon rind, the chopped parsley, the dried thyme, the minced bay leaves, and a pinch of powdered cloves) which have previously been made up. Then put in the casserole a layer of the quartered small onions. Repeat the layers in the order above given, until all the pieces of rabbit have been used.

Next pour over the contents of the casserole the marinade, to which you have added the mushroom catsup (this is sometimes a little hard to come by, but Crosse & Blackwell's bottled Mushroom Sauce can be substituted) and enough beef bouillon so that the marinade will barely cover the contents of the casserole. Cover the casserole, and seal with a flour and water paste, so that no steam will escape. Put the casserole in a 300-degree oven for about 1½ hours.

At the end of the cooking time, unseal the casserole and take up the rabbit pieces and onions, and keep them hot. Strain the remaining liquid into a saucepan, bring it to a quick boil, then reduce the flame. Put the liver, which has been previously sautéed in 1 tablespoon of butter for about 1 minute, through a sieve into the sauce.

(At this point, if you have used a wild rabbit and collected the blood, slowly heat the blood, mix it with 3 or 4 tablespoons of sauce, and then stir it into the sauce.)

Add to the sauce the port wine and the currant jelly, blend well, and pour the sauce over the rabbit and onions. This is really a magnificent dish, and serves 3 to 4.

One of the best known German dishes is *Hassenpfeffer*.

Hasenpfeffer is, of course, a spicy dish, and after you have eaten it, you'll understand the old Pennsylvania Dutch saying, *"Do is 's wo d'r haws im pef'r sitst"* (here is where the rabbit sits in the pepper). As you will see, you had better start this dish a couple of days before you plan to serve it.

HASENPFEFFER

1 *large rabbit (or 2 small ones)*	1 *tsp. mustard seed*
2 *cups dry red wine*	½ *tsp. thyme*
2 *cups tarragon vinegar*	5 *whole cloves*
2 *onions*	4 *tbsp. olive oil*
1 *carrot*	*Juice 2 lemons*
2 *whole allspice*	2 *tbsp. chopped parsley*
3 *bay leaves*	*Bacon drippings*
1 *tbsp. salt*	¼ *lb. diced raw ham*
1 *tsp. black pepper*	5 *little green onions*
	Consommé (if necessary)

Disjoint a large dressed rabbit (or 2 small ones) and put the pieces in an earthenware crock or enamel bowl. Cover with the following marinade: 2 cups of dry California red wine, 2 cups of tarragon vinegar, 2 large onions, peeled and sliced, 1 carrot, sliced, 2 whole allspice, crushed, 3 bay leaves, 1 tablespoon of salt, 1 teaspoon of black pepper, 1 teaspoon of mustard seed, ½ teaspoon of thyme, 5 whole cloves, 4 tablespoons of olive oil, the juice of 2 lemons, and 2 tablespoons of chopped parsley. Let marinate for 2 days, turning the meat occasionally.

Meantime, melt 2 tablespoons bacon drippings in skillet and add ¼ pound of diced raw ham. Brown it lightly, then remove the ham to a Dutch oven or a pot with a heavy lid. In the same fat, brown 5 little green onions, chopped, and then put them in the pot with the ham. Next, brown the rabbit pieces (which have been drained and rolled in flour) in the same fat, adding more, if necessary. Then add the browned rabbit to the ham and the browned onions, and pour the marinade over them. It should just cover the rabbit. If it doesn't, add more red wine, and consommé, in equal parts. Cover the pot, and simmer until the rabbit is very tender—about 2 hours.

To serve, remove the rabbit to a platter, strain the gravy, skimming off any excess fat, and serve separately. Or you can serve the whole thing as is, which is the way I prefer it.

Here is a recipe for rabbit in the Hungarian manner.

RABBIT PAPRIKA

1 *tender young rabbit, disjointed*	3 *medium-sized onions*
Salt	1½ *tbsp. Rosen paprika*
Pepper	1 *clove garlic, minced*
Flour	2 *fresh tomatoes*
4 *tbsp. butter*	½ *cup dry sherry*
	1 *cup sour cream*

Cut a tender young rabbit into serving pieces, and rub them well with salt and pepper, then roll them in flour.

In a heavy iron skillet or a Dutch oven melt 4 tablespoons of butter, and add 3 medium-sized onions, peeled and chopped. Let these cook very slowly for about 30 minutes, watching carefully to see that they don't burn. Then add 1½ tablespoons of Rosen paprika, and cook for another 15 minutes, stirring constantly.

Now add the rabbit pieces, 1 clove of garlic, minced, 2 fresh tomatoes, cut up, and ½ cup of dry sherry. Cover the skillet and let all this simmer for about an hour, or until the rabbit is tender.

Just a few minutes before serving, add 1 cup of sour cream to the rabbit. Mix it in well, correct for seasoning, and let everything simmer just long enough to heat the sour cream. Serve hot.

The three most common ways of cooking venison are broiling, making a ragout, and roasting. The following recipe was given me by an old friend who never misses going after deer during the hunting season. He is not only an excellent shot, but a damn good game cook, and is much sought after as a companion on any hunting trip.

ROAST HAUNCH OF VENISON

6- to 7-lb. haunch venison	2 cups dry red wine
5 tbsp. butter	Olive oil
1 large onion, chopped	Salt
2 tbsp. chopped little green onions	Freshly ground pepper
2 large carrots, chopped	½ lb. salt pork
4 whole cloves	2 cloves garlic
½ tsp. thyme	1 cup red currant jelly
½ tsp. marjoram	Pinch powdered ginger
½ tsp. tarragon	Pinch powdered cloves
½ tsp. basil	1 tsp. lemon juice
½ tsp. rosemary	¼ cup sour cream
	Flour (if necessary)
1 tbsp. brandy	

First, marinate the meat. The standard marinade at many hunt clubs is ⅔ red wine and ⅓ water, to which generous seasonings of pepper, bay leaves, thyme, tarragon, and mustard seed have been added. But here's a better one that dates back to the seventeenth century. Fry out 1 large mild onion, chopped, 2 tablespoons of chopped little green onions, and 2 large carrots, chopped, in 5 tablespoons of butter. Add 4 whole cloves, ½ teaspoon each of thyme, marjoram, tarragon, basil, and rosemary. Add 1 cup of red wine. Then put everything through a coarse sieve. Now brush the venison with olive oil, dust with plenty of freshly ground pepper and salt, and pour the marinade over the venison and let it soak in it for about 8 hours.

To cook, lard the venison generously with salt pork and insert slivers of garlic into the meat. Roast in a 450-degree oven, 20 to 30 minutes to the pound, basting frequently with the drippings and the marinade, which has been added. When the meat is tender, remove from the roasting pan but keep in a warm oven while making the gravy.

And now the gravy! In the roasting pan slowly melt 1 cup of red currant jelly with the drippings and the marinade, to which 1 cup of red wine has been added.

While this is simmering, add a pinch of powdered ginger, a pinch of powdered clove, and 1 teaspoon of lemon juice. When the gravy has thickened and reduced a little, slowly add ¼ cup of sour cream and blend everything thoroughly. If you prefer the gravy a little thicker, sprinkle in a little flour, being sure no lumps form. Just before serving, add 1 tablespoon of good brandy, and pour into the gravy boat.

TENDERLOIN OF VENISON SMITANE

6 tenderloin of venison	Pinch caraway seeds
6 strips of bacon	½ cup dry white wine
¼ lb. butter	1½ cups cream
1 medium-sized onion	½ pint sour cream
4 large mushrooms	Salt
2 bay leaves	Freshly ground pepper
Pinch thyme	Dash Worcestershire sauce

Juice ½ lemon

Wrap 6 tenderloin of venison in 6 strips of bacon, and pan broil over a medium flame for about 6 minutes on each side. Then put them in a warm oven while the sauce is being prepared.

Place ¼ pound of butter in a saucepan with 1 medium-sized onion cut julienne, 4 large mushrooms, also cut julienne, 2 bay leaves, and a pinch each of thyme and caraway seeds. Let this simmer for a little while—say three or four minutes—then add ½ cup of dry California white wine. Continue to simmer until the onions and mushrooms are tender; then add 1½ cups of cream, and let it simmer for about 20 minutes more. Remove from fire and add 1 cup of sour cream, salt and freshly ground pepper to taste, a dash of Worcestershire sauce, and the juice of ½ lemon. Reheat.

Serve the tenderloin of venison with this sauce poured over them.

8. POULTRY

I know of no other animal or bird that is more of a cosmopolitan than our barnyard friend, the chicken. From earliest times, the chicken has been served on the tables of almost every nation under the sun, and certainly no other edible is so universally admired.

Poultry is for the cook what canvas is for the painter. There are as many nuances of flavor as there are of color. Chicken can be boiled, roasted, fried, stewed, grilled; it can be served hot or cold, whole or in part, with or without sauces, boned or stuffed.

In the Bois de Boulogne in Paris there are some of the finest restaurants in the world. In the middle of the Bois, resting against a beautiful natural waterfall, was the Pavillon de la Cascade. It was an enchanting place to lunch before going to the races, which were just around the corner at Auteuil. And one of their most delicious dishes was Chicken *à la Chasseur*. This is the way it was made.

CHICKEN À LA CHASSEUR

1 *young chicken, 2-2½ lb.*	2 *young green onions*
Salt	1 *oz. brandy*
Pepper	1 *cup dry white wine*
Lemon juice	2 *fresh tomatoes*
1 *tbsp. butter*	½ *cup chicken broth*

1 tbsp. olive oil   1 tbsp. minced parsley
10 medium-sized mushrooms   Pinch tarragon

Joint a tender young chicken, rub the pieces with lemon juice, and sprinkle them with salt and pepper, freshly ground. In a heavy iron skillet put 1 tablespoon each of butter and good olive oil. When this is hot, put in the chicken pieces and sauté over a medium flame until they are golden brown on all sides. Then add 10 medium-sized mushrooms, and let cook for 5 minutes. Now add 2 finely chopped young green onions (including tops), 1 ounce of brandy, 1 cup of dry California white wine, 2 fresh tomatoes, skinned, peeled and chopped, ½ cup of chicken broth, and 1 tablespoon of minced parsley. Cover the skillet, and let it cook over a gentle fire for about 25 minutes, or until the chicken is tender. Before serving, sprinkle a pinch of tarragon over it.

With this dish, crusty French bread is a "must," as is also a bottle of fine dry California white wine. Wild rice and tiny string beans go along excellently, and a salad of fresh tossed greens with a mild dressing.

One hundred and forty-eight years ago, in the vicinity of a little village in Piedmont, in Northern Italy, a famous French dish was invented by a battlefield chef of Napoleon Bonaparte, which became known as *Le Poulet Marengo*.

Actually, Chicken Marengo starts out as fried chicken —a delicacy in any man's language—and takes on other culinary delights as it progresses. To be perfectly honest, I wasn't present at the inception of the dish; but here's my version of it, and I think even Napoleon would go for it.

CHICKEN MARENGO

2 2½-lb. broilers   1½ cups sliced fresh mush-
Flour   rooms
Salt   2 tsp. minced parsley
Pepper   4 tomatoes
¼ cup olive oil   1 cup dry white wine

4 *small white onions*	1 *tbsp. brandy*
1 *small clove garlic*	1 *tbsp. tomato paste*
	1 *tbsp. flour*

Wash and clean two 2½-pound broilers, then cut them up as for frying and dust the pieces lightly with seasoned flour. In a large skillet heat ¼ cup olive oil, and sauté the chicken until it is golden brown, turning frequently so that all the pieces are done evenly. Then remove the chicken and keep warm.

In the same skillet put 4 peeled and chopped small white onions, 1 small clove of garlic, crushed, 1½ cups of sliced fresh mushrooms, 2 teaspoons of minced parsley, and, if necessary, a little more olive oil. Cook this mixture until the mushrooms are tender; then add 4 sliced and peeled tomatoes, 1 cup of dry California white wine, 1 tablespoon of brandy, 1 tablespoon of tomato paste, and 1 tablespoon of flour. Mix and blend the ingredients well, and allow to simmer over a medium flame for about 10 minutes. Now put the chicken in the sauce, cover the pan, and cook for about 30 minutes, or until the chicken is completely tender. Serve in the sauce.

The Italians have a way with chickens, too. One of the best-known Italian chicken dishes is Chicken *Cacciatore,* which is chicken, hunters' style.

CHICKEN CACCIATORE

2 *tender chickens* (*about*	2 *small green peppers*
2 *lb. each*)	2 *slices canned pimento*
Flour	2 *cups canned tomatoes*
Salt	1 *tbsp. tomato paste*
Pepper	2 *tbsp. chopped parsley*
1½ *oz. butter*	*Generous pinch thyme*
2½ *oz. pure olive oil*	*Generous pinch oregano*
1 *large clove garlic*	1 *cup dry red wine*
2 *medium-sized onions*	2 *cups sliced mushrooms*

Cut 2 tender chickens (about 2 pounds each) into serving pieces and shake them in a paper bag of seasoned flour.

In a heavy skillet put 1½ ounces of butter, 2½ ounces of pure olive oil, and a large clove of garlic, minced. When the fat is hot, add the chicken pieces along with 2 medium-sized onions, peeled and chopped, and 2 small green peppers, seeded and chopped. Sauté until the chicken pieces are a nice golden brown. Then add to the skillet 2 slices of canned pimento, chopped, 2 cups of canned tomatoes (the Italian variety if you live near an Italian grocery store), 1 tablespoon of tomato paste, salt and pepper to taste, 2 tablespoons chopped parsley, a generous pinch each of thyme and oregano, and 1 cup of dry California red wine (or an American Chianti). Cover and simmer gently for about 1 hour. Then add 2 cups of thinly sliced mushrooms, and continue simmering, covered, for about 30 minutes longer, or until chicken is tender. Serve as hot as possible, with spaghetti *al burro,* which is plain boiled spaghetti well buttered.

We have used the following chicken dish frequently for informal entertaining, and it always rates raves. It was devised by an old and dear friend who lives in Walnut Creek, in California, Orleanne Harvey, and I have named it Chicken Orleanne. It is a grand entree for a party of four, and can be prepared in advance.

CHICKEN ORLEANNE

3 *large chicken legs*	*Parsley, chopped*
3 *large chicken thighs*	*Rosemary seasoning powder*
2 *large chicken breasts*	1 *stalk celery*
Fresh lime juice	3 *medium-sized carrots*
Salt	5 *small white onions*
Freshly ground pepper	½ *cup dry white wine*
Seasoned flour	1 15½-*oz. can cream of*
4 *oz. butter*	*mushroom soup*
Clove garlic	*Paprika*

Get 3 large chicken legs and thighs and two large breasts, dividing the legs and thighs, and halving the breasts.

Brush the pieces with fresh lime juice, season with salt and freshly ground pepper, and shake in a bag of seasoned flour. Sauté the chicken pieces in a heavy skillet in the butter until they are a golden brown (about 20 minutes).

Next, place a layer of chicken pieces in a casserole, and sprinkle the layer with ½ clove of garlic, minced, a generous pinch of parsley, and 2 light sprinkles of rosemary seasoning powder. Then add a second layer of chicken pieces, and repeat the seasonings on that layer. Then sprinkle over the chicken pieces the stalk of celery, chopped, and lay over and around the top the medium-sized carrots, sliced in half lengthwise, and the little white onions.

Into the skillet the chicken was sautéed in pour the dry white wine, and blend it well with the butter remaining in the skillet. Then add the cream of mushroom soup, and again blend the contents of the skillet. Then pour this sauce over the contents of the casserole, sprinkle the top lightly with freshly ground pepper and paprika, put into a moderate oven (285-300 degrees) and bake for 2 hours. Serve from the casserole.

A wonderful chicken dish that one sometimes encounters on the menus of fine restaurants is Chicken Sauté Sec (sec being French for "dry"). But, strangely enough, the recipe is almost impossible to find in cookbooks. But fortunately I found an excellent recipe in a brochure put out by the Wine Advisory Board in San Francisco, and I am delighted to present it herewith.

CHICKEN SAUTÉ SEC

1 3½-lb. frying chicken cut in pieces	4 tbsp. butter
	2 tbsp. chopped parsley
2 shallots (or little green onions)	Pinch dried thyme
	Pinch dried basil
½ cup California dry white wine	Flour
	Salt
1 4-oz. can sliced mushrooms	Pepper

Dust the chicken pieces with flour and season with salt and pepper. Melt the butter in a large heavy skillet, add the chicken pieces, and sauté until they are golden brown on all sides. If necessary, add a little more butter to the skillet. Next add the finely chopped shallots (or little green onions, bulbs and tops), chopped parsley, the dried thyme and basil, and the dry white wine (a good California sauterne, Chablis, or White Pinot). Cover the skillet tightly and simmer gently for 30 minutes. Then uncover and add the drained sliced mushrooms (or ¼ pound of sliced fresh mushrooms which have been sautéd in a tablespoon or so of butter for about 6 minutes). Continue cooking for about 15 minutes, or until the chicken is tender and no liquid remains in the pan. This recipe serves 3 to 4.

Another way of cooking chicken that's hard to beat is broiling it. But leave it to the French to think up a different way of broiling chicken—with a basting agent of chopped chicken giblets and white wine.

BROILED CHICKEN AU VIN BLANC

2 fryers (about 1½ pounds each)	1 cup very dry white wine
1 small onion, diced	Clove garlic
1 tbsp. chopped parsley	Lime juice
Pinch of thyme	Salt
Pinch of marjoram	Freshly ground pepper
1 cup cold water	2 tbsp. butter
	Flour

Have 2 fryers (about 1½ pounds each) split for broiling. Cut off the necks.

Put the necks and the giblets in a saucepan with 1 small onion, peeled and diced, 1 tablespoon of chopped parsley, a generous pinch each of thyme and marjoram, and 1 cup of cold water. Cover, and let simmer until tender, then add 1 cup of very dry California white wine (a Chablis or Riesling). Strain and reserve the liquid. Chop the giblets fine, and set aside.

Rub the chickens with a cut of clove of garlic, sprinkle

with lime juice, salt and freshly ground pepper, and brush with soft butter. Then place the halves, skin side down, in a shallow pan and place low under the broiler. Turn occasionally, and baste frequently with the wine stock. When the chickens are well browned and tender (about 30 minutes), remove from the pan, add chopped giblets, and thicken the remaining wine sauce with a little flour blended with soft butter. Heat, pour sauce over the chicken, and serve.

Dijon is the capital of the department of Côte-d'Or, whence come the greatest Burgundies in the world. Dijon is also well known for its mustard and for the black currant liquor called Cassis de Dijon. It is a gastronomical center as well as a wine center, and its restaurants are famous all over Europe.

Coq au Chambertin is a specialty at all Dijon's fine restaurants. The preparation of this exalted chicken dish runs contrary to the usual rule of white wines with chicken dishes. When you prepare it, use a fine California Burgundy.

COQ AU CHAMBERTIN

2 *young chickens* (2 *to* 2½ *pounds each*)	*Flour*
	2 *oz. butter*
Salt	⅛ *lb. bacon*
Paprika	12 *tiny onions*
Nutmeg	2 *cloves garlic*
Freshly ground pepper	¼ *tsp. thyme*
1 *tbsp. chopped parsley*	¼ *tsp. marjoram*
Leaves from 1 *stalk celery*	¼ *tsp. rosemary*
½ *cup sliced mushrooms*	1 *bay leaf*
3 *cups California Burgundy*	3 *oz. brandy*

Disjoint 2 young chickens (2 to 2½ pounds each) and rub the pieces well with salt, freshly ground pepper, paprika, and a little nutmeg, and then dredge them with flour.

In a skillet melt 2 ounces of butter, then add 2 ounces

of lean bacon (⅛ pound), diced. When the bacon has browned lightly remove and set it aside.

Put the chicken pieces into the fat in the skillet, and lightly brown them on all sides. Then add 12 tiny onions, peeled, 2 crushed cloves of garlic, ¼ teaspoon each of thyme, rosemary, and marjoram, 1 minced bay leaf, 1 tablespoon chopped parsley, the green leaves from a stalk of celery, chopped fine, and ½ cup of sliced mushrooms. Let all simmer for about 5 minutes, then pour over the mixture 3 ounces of brandy, and ignite. When the flame has burned out, transfer the contents of the skillet to a casserole, add the diced bacon, and 3 cups of California Burgundy. Cover the casserole and seal with a thick flour-and-water paste, put into a moderate oven (325 degrees), and cook for 2 hours.

Unseal the casserole, and reduce the gravy, as desired, with additional red wine, or thicken with equal parts of flour and soft butter, blended together.

Niu Moa Ai, chicken baked in a coconut, to my way of thinking, is one of the outstanding triumphs of gastronomy, from the standpoint of both flavor and service. Served in your home, it will be a topic of conversation among your guests for a long, long time. It requires no ingredient that is not available in almost any grocery and meat market, and it is not difficult at all to prepare and cook.

NIU MOA AI
(Chicken Baked in Coconut)

1 *spring chicken*	6 *small tomatoes*
4 *fresh coconuts*	1 *tsp. brown sugar*
5 *slices bacon*	1 *clove garlic*
Salt	*Dash of tabasco*
Pepper, freshly ground	2 *ears fresh corn*
1 *large onion*	4 *small bay leaves*
1 *green pepper*	4 *tbsp. dry white wine*

Disjoint a spring chicken, and remove the skin. Dice 5 slices of bacon and fry out in a skillet, then lightly brown the chicken pieces in the bacon fat after sprinkling them with salt and freshly ground pepper. Take the chicken out, remove all the meat from the bones, dice it and set it aside. Next, chop a large, peeled onion and a seeded green pepper, and lightly brown them in the bacon fat. Then add 6 small tomatoes, which have been stewed with 1 teaspoon of brown sugar, salt and pepper to taste, a small clove of garlic, minced, and a dash of Tabasco. Cook until the mixture thickens.

In the meantime, you will have taken the tops off 4 fresh coconuts by sawing them through at a point about ¼ of the way down. Remove half the meat from the coconuts by scraping it away in shreds. Shave the corn from 2 ears and mix it with the coconut meat, moistening it with a small amount of the coconut milk. When the onion-pepper-tomato mixture has thickened, remove it from the fire and mix it well into the coconut meat and corn, then add the diced chicken meat, and again mix everything well. Fill the coconuts two thirds full with the mixture and add a small crumbled bay leaf and a tablespoon of white wine to each.

Now replace the tops on the coconuts, and seal the joinings tightly with a thick flour-and-water paste. Set the coconuts in a roasting pan, with about an inch of water on the bottom (or in the depressions of a large muffin tin), and bake in a medium oven (about 375 degrees) for 45 minutes to an hour. If the outer shells of the coconuts should tend to scorch, baste them occasionally with the water in the bottom of the pan. After having removed the tops, serve one coconut to each individual. If the coconuts are small, and there is more of the chicken mixture than will fill them, put the remaining mixture in a greased baking dish, and set in the oven along with the coconuts. This will provide "seconds" for the guests who have emptied their coconuts.

This is a magnificent dish, and, incidentally, an ideal one to serve to guests who have a tendency to be late, for the contents, if coconut is not unsealed, will remain hot for 4 or 5 hours.

The classic chicken dish of old Russia is Chicken Kiev,

or *Côtelettes Kiev* (*côtelettes* is French for cutlets),
or Breast of Chicken, Kiev. It is a very swank dish,
usually found only on the menus of expensive restaurants.

Of course, different chefs have different versions of the
dish, but I think the following recipe, which I devised, is
the most savory of any I have ever tasted.

BREAST OF CHICKEN KIEV

3 *large chicken breasts*	2 *tbsp. chopped parsley*
6 *mushrooms, finely*	*Salt*
chopped	*Pepper*
Butter	2 *eggs*
½ *lb. sweet butter*	1 *tbsp. vodka*
1 *clove garlic*	*Fine bread crumbs*

Remove the bones and skin from 3 large chicken breasts,
and cut away all gristle (or have the butcher do this for
you). Separate the 2 halves of each breast, making 6
half breasts. Place each half breast between 2 sheets of
waxed paper, and flatten with the flat side of a cleaver or
a wooden mallet. They should somewhat resemble thin
pancakes.

Sauté the finely chopped mushrooms in 1 tablespoon
of butter for about 5 minutes, or until tender.

Let ½ pound of sweet (unsalted) butter come to about
room temperature. Then cream together the sweet butter,
the clove of garlic, finely minced, the chopped parsley,
and the sautéed chopped mushrooms until smooth. Chill
in the refrigerator until firm enough to handle, then shape
the seasoned butter into 6 oval rolls about 2½ to 3
inches long and ¾ to 1 inch wide at the thickest part.
Place these rolls into water with ice, and let them remain
until hard.

Sprinkle a very little salt and pepper on each flattened
half breast of chicken. Remove the butter rolls from the
water and ice, quickly dry each, and place 1 roll on each
of the flattened chicken breasts. Roll the chicken around
the butter roll, folding the ends in so that the butter rolls
are completely encased. Watch this carefully, because if
the rolls are not completely encased, the butter will leak

out as it melts, and all your work has gone for naught. Secure the rolled chicken breasts with wooden toothpicks.

Lightly beat 2 eggs with the vodka. Roll the rolled-up chicken breasts in fine bread crumbs, then in the beaten eggs, and again in bread crumbs. Fry in plenty of butter until the rolls are golden brown, making certain that the butter they are fried in is not too hot, because if it is, the outside of the rolls will brown before the chicken has a chance to cook thoroughly. When the rolls are golden brown, drain them on paper toweling, and place in a hot oven for about 5 minutes. Serve at once.

This chicken dish is a work of art, and one of the most delicious I have ever tasted, yet simple to prepare.

CHICKEN LEGS À LA DRENNAN

4 complete chicken legs	Pinch finely chopped leaf
Seasoned flour	sage
3 oz. butter	½ tsp. chili powder
Pinch dried marjoram	Paprika
Pinch dried thyme	1 cup chopped parsley
½ cup dry white wine	

In a heavy and rather deep iron skillet, melt the butter. Then add a pinch each of marjoram, thyme, and finely chopped leaf sage, the chili powder, and a generous sprinkling of paprika. Blend all these ingredients thoroughly with the melted butter, stirring with a fork.

Toss the chicken legs (legs and thighs separated) in a bag of seasoned flour and then put them in the skillet with the seasoned butter and brown them on both sides over a fairly brisk flame or medium high heat. Then turn the flame or heat down to the lowest point, cover the skillet, and let the chicken legs slowly simmer for anywhere from 45 minutes to an hour, or until tender. Then remove the chicken legs to a platter and put them in a warm oven.

To the juices in the skillet add the chopped parsley and very dry American white wine. Stir and blend everything well, and when hot pour over the chicken legs and serve.

I have avidly eaten curry dishes devised and cooked by Hindus and Dutchmen. In all immodesty, I think that my lamb curry is tops. But the finest chicken (and lobster) curry that I have ever eaten was prepared for the Little Woman and me by Max Guggiari, of the Imperial House in Chicago. He gave me the recipe, and permission to use it, so I pass it on here. Believe me, the service of this dish will make you a prince among hosts, or a princess among hostesses.

CAPON AND LOBSTER CURRY

1 lb. cooked lobster meat	1 stalk celery
1 lb. cooked white meat, chicken or capon	2 bay leaves
	3 oz. flour
¼ lb. butter	2 oz. curry powder
1 apple	1 qt. chicken broth
1 large onion	1 cup cream
1 coconut, milk and meat	

Melt ¼ pound of butter in a very large skillet, and fry 1 apple, cored, peeled, and sliced; 1 large onion, peeled and sliced; 1 stalk of celery, cut up; and 2 bay leaves; and smother this mixture for 15 minutes. Then sprinkle 3 ounces of flour and 2 ounces of the best curry powder in the mixture. Stir well, and cook slowly for another 15 minutes. Now add 1 quart of chicken broth, 1 cup of cream, the milk and the shredded meat from the coconut, and again cook slowly for another 15 minutes. Remove from the fire and strain the sauce through a coarse piece of cheesecloth or a fine sieve into a large saucepan, and add 1 pound each of cooked lobster meat and the cooked white meat of a chicken or capon. The pieces of the lobster meat and the white meat of the fowl should be about 1 inch square. Season to taste with salt and pepper, and let the curry heat thoroughly over a very low flame. Serve over rice, and put a generous tablespoon of chutney over each serving. This amount of curry could serve five or six people, but you'd better count on its serving only four.

One of the most exciting dishes in Spanish or Mexican cuisine is the justly famous *Arroz con Pollo*. The English translation of this is rice with chicken, but *"pollo"* means a young and tender chicken, and not an old barnyard habitué. Garlic is normally used in this dish, but I think the little green onions give it a more delicate flavor. That's really a concession from me, a passionate devotée of garlic!

ARROZ CON POLLO

2 *young chickens*	1 *green pepper*
Lime juice	1 *sweet red pepper*
Salt	2 *tbsp. chopped parsley*
Pepper	1 *bay leaf*
¼ *cup olive oil*	¼ *tsp. saffron*
¼ *lb. lean raw ham*	2 *cups chicken broth*
6 *little green onions*	2 *cups long-grain raw rice*
4 *large tomatoes*	2 *oz. Madeira*

Cut 2 young tender chickens into serving pieces, brush with lime juice, season with salt and freshly ground pepper, and put in the refrigerator for about 2 hours.

Heat ¼ cut of pure olive oil in a heavy skillet or Dutch oven, and when smoking hot, put in the chicken pieces and lightly brown on all sides. Then add ¼ pound of diced lean raw ham, and 6 little green onions (bulb and tops), chopped. When the onion begins to brown, add 4 large tomatoes, peeled and quartered, 1 green and red pepper, each seeded and chopped, 2 tablespoons chopped parsley, salt and pepper to taste, 1 bay leaf, crumbled, and ¼ teaspoon of powdered saffron. Mix all these ingredients well and simmer for about 5 minutes; then add 2 cups of boiling chicken broth, and simmer, closely covered.

When the chicken is nearly tender add 2 cups of long-grain rice which has been washed in several changes of water and well drained. Cover again, and simmer gently for about 30 minutes.

When the chicken is tender and the rice is cooked (it should have absorbed most of the juices), add 2 ounces of Madeira.

If you've cooked this dish in an earthenware casserole, serve it, as is, on the table. If not, make a mound of the rice on a very hot platter, and surround it with the chicken pieces. If you really want to go to town, sauté at least 2 dozen medium-sized mushroom caps in butter and a little sherry, and border the chicken with them, and then lay some pimento strips across the rice.

Paella is the second classic Spanish chicken dish, and in addition to chicken it calls for shellfish.

Somerset Maugham knew *Paella* as *Arroz À la Valenciana,* and he fell in love with it. A number of great chefs have devised their own version of this wonderful dish. Well, who am I to be left out of the parade! So here is my version of *Arroz À la Valenciana* with not only chicken and clams, but lobster and savory vegetables. It may sound a little formidable, and it is work, but I don't believe anyone who makes and eats it will say that it wasn't worth the trouble.

ARROZ À LA VALENCIANA

2 broiling chickens, quartered
Salt and pepper
Paprika
Powdered ginger
½ cup olive oil
½ lb. bacon
2 onions
2 green peppers
3 tomatoes
3 cloves garlic

2 lobsters (1½ to 2 lbs. each)
1 #2 can artichoke hearts
2 cups long-grain rice
Hot chicken broth (about 4 cups in all)
24 small clams
12 1-inch pieces of Italian sausage
1 tsp. saffron powder
½ cup dry white wine

Quarter the broilers, and rub them with salt, pepper, paprika, and powdered ginger.

In a heavy iron pot, or Dutch oven, or casserole, put the olive oil, and the bacon, diced. When sizzling, add the chicken pieces, and sauté until they are golden brown on all sides. Remove them and keep warm, and to the pot add the lobsters, cut in pieces, and when they are well sautéed, remove them and keep warm.

To the pot add the onions, chopped, and the green peppers, chopped. When the onions begin to brown, add the tomatoes, cut in pieces, and the artichoke hearts, drained. Cook for about 5 minutes, then add to the pot 2 cups of long-grain rice, well washed. Stir from time to time to keep the rice from burning, and cook until the rice begins to take on color and dry out a little.

Return the chicken pieces and the lobster pieces to the pot, and pour in 1 cup of hot chicken broth. When this is absorbed, add another cup of hot chicken broth. Simmer until the chicken and rice are nearly tender.

Now add to the pot 24 small clams in their shells, which have been well scrubbed, and about 12 1-inch pieces of Italian sausage. If necessary, add more hot chicken broth, depending on the state of the rice.

In a mortar (or heavy bowl) put the 3 cloves of garlic, sliced, the teaspoon of saffron, and about 6 ounces of hot chicken broth. With a pestle (or a muddler) grind the garlic and mix well, until the broth is thoroughly impregnated with the garlic and saffron. Then strain the broth into the pot, and add the dry white wine, and correct the seasoning with salt and pepper.

When the rice is properly cooked (enough of the hot chicken broth having been added to complete the cooking), each kernel of rice should be separate, and not of a mushy consistency. The clams will have opened their shells, and the chicken and lobster will be tender to the fork. Serve from the pot, or casserole in which the dish has been cooked, to 6 or 8.

A real, old-fashioned chicken pie is a work of art, and nothing can touch it to my way of thinking. Somehow, it sort of takes me back to my grandmother's farm, where it was a frequently served dish, made with freshly killed chickens, garden fresh vegetables, and thick cream. If

you've ever eaten the dish out in the country, I think
this version will have a nostalgic effect on you.

OLD FASHIONED CHICKEN PIE

1 4- to 5-lb. stewing hen
1 cup dry white wine
Water
1 large onion
3 stalks celery
1 sprig parsley
1 bay leaf
6 peppercorns
Pinch dried marjoram
12 small white onions
1 pkg. frozen baby lima
    beans

6 small carrots
½ lb. fresh mushrooms
2 tbsp. butter
2 tbsp. flour
1 tsp. Worcestershire sauce
1 tsp. grated lemon rind
2 egg yolks
½ cup cream
Rich pastry crust
1 egg
2 tbsp. cream
Salt
Pepper

Cut the stewing hen into pieces. Put into a pot, add the
dry white wine and enough water to cover. Also add 1
large onion, peeled and cut in quarters, stalks of celery
(and leaves), sprig of parsley, bay leaf, peppercorns,
pinch of dried marjoram, and 2 teaspoons of salt. Bring
to a boil, then lower the flame and simmer for about 2
hours, or until the chicken is tender. Let the chicken
cool in the broth. Then take the chicken pieces out, remove the skin, and separate the meat from the bones,
cutting it in fairly good-sized pieces. Then strain the
broth and reserve, discarding the solids.

Boil the whole tiny white onions and small carrots in
a little salted water for about 15 to 20 minutes, or until
just tender. Also cook a package of frozen baby lima
beans according to directions on package.

In a saucepan sauté the sliced fresh mushrooms in
the butter for about 6 minutes. Then blend in the flour,
and add 2 cups of the strained chicken broth, the Worcestershire sauce, and grated lemon rind. Cook, stirring
constantly, until it thickens. Beat the egg yolks with the
cream, take the saucepan off the fire, add salt and pepper

to taste if necessary, and stir this into the mushroom sauce.

Arrange the tiny onions, the carrots (cut in 1-inch pieces), the baby lima beans, and the chicken meat in a casserole or baking dish, and pour the mushroom sauce over all. Cover the casserole with a rich pie crust, slitting the top of the dough before baking to allow the steam to escape. Brush the dough with a mixture of 1 egg slightly beaten with 2 tablespoons of cream to give the crust a rich color when done. Place in a 425-degree oven until crust is golden brown, about 25 minutes. This recipe will serve about 6.

My nomination for the Number 1 luncheon dish is Plantation Chicken Shortcake. All you need is some cooked or boned chicken, some corn bread mix, some mushrooms, and a little grated Parmesan cheese.

PLANTATION CHICKEN SHORTCAKE

Sliced breasts cold chicken	*1 cup cream*
Slices baked ham	*2 tbsp. sherry*
Corn bread squares	*1 tbsp. flour*
½ pound mushrooms	*Salt*
3 tbsp. butter	*White pepper*
Grated Parmesan cheese	

First make a mushroom sauce. Clean ½ pound of small mushrooms (or large ones cut in quarters) and lightly brown them in a saucepan with 2 tablespoons of butter. Add 1 cup of cream and 2 tablespoons of sherry, and cook 6 to 8 minutes. Thicken with about a tablespoon of butter mixed with a tablespoon of flour, and season with ½ teaspoon of salt and a little white pepper.

Now take pieces of corn bread about 3 inches square (you can buy the corn bread at the corner bakery, or you can make it yourself out of a prepared corn bread mix so easily you won't believe it) and split and butter them. Place them in a large shallow baking dish, and lay on each piece a thin slice of baked ham. Over the ham lay a slice of cold chicken (preferably white meat). Next, pour your mushroom sauce over the combination, sprinkle grated Parmesan cheese over the top, and put the dish under the broiler and let it cook until it is hot and bubbly.

Chicken livers make an ideal light luncheon dish, and they can be made into a savory main course dinner dish.

The following dish is an ideal one for a Sunday brunch, along with scrambled eggs, grilled link sausages, and hot biscuits.

CHICKEN LIVERS IN SOUR CREAM

1 lb. chicken livers
2 oz. butter (4 tbsp.)
1 green pepper, minced
2 tbsp. flour
½ pint sour cream
¼ cup chicken broth

1 4-oz. can mushroom stems
  and pieces, drained
2 tbsp. chopped parsley
1 tbsp. grated onion
Salt
Pepper

½ tsp. Ac'cent

Cut the chicken livers in half, and gently sauté them in a large skillet with the butter, turning frequently, for about 5 minutes. Remove livers. Sauté the minced green pepper in same pan for 5 minutes. Sprinkle the flour over green pepper and stir well. Add commercial sour cream and chicken broth. Cook, stirring constantly, until mixture boils and thickens. Then add the mushroom stems and pieces, drained, chopped parsley, grated onion, salt and pepper to taste, and the Ac'cent. Just before serving, add livers to sauce and heat gently, but thoroughly. Serves 4 to 6.

Stuffed fowls are exceedingly popular among the people of the Near East. In "The Book of the Thousand Nights and a Night" (*The Arabian Nights*) mention is frequently made of fowls stuffed with pistachio nuts, and modern Near East cooks still use this delicate nut for flavoring. So suppose we call the following dish Turkey Scheherazade, in honor of the heroine of the Arabian Nights!

TURKEY SCHEHERAZADE

1 10- to 12-lb. turkey
Olive oil
¼ tsp. powdered ginger

Stuffing

½ cup raw rice	Chopped giblets
2 tbsp. butter	½ cup seedless raisins
1 large onion	½ tsp. dried thyme
2 stalks celery	¼ tsp. dried sage
6 cups bread crumbs	1 tbsp. chopped parsley
Dry sherry wine	Salt
1 cup pistachio nuts	Freshly ground pepper

1 beaten egg

Gravy

¼ cup pan drippings	1 cup dry white wine
¼ cup flour	Salt
1 cup water	Pepper

Rub the inside and out of the turkey with olive oil, then rub the inside with about ¼ teaspoon of powdered ginger. Boil the giblets in water (except the liver) about 1 hour, or until tender. Add the liver to the boiling giblets about 8 minutes before the cooking time is up. Also cook the rice in your favorite manner, so that it will be fluffy and tender.

In a saucepan melt the butter, and when hot add the sliced onion and chopped celery. Sauté these until the onion takes on a little color.

In a large bowl combine the day-old bread, cubed, which has previously been moistened with dry sherry wine, the sautéed onions and celery, the pistachio nuts, the boiled rice, the chopped giblets, the seedless raisins, dried thyme, dried sage, chopped parsley, salt and freshly ground pepper to taste, and the beaten egg. Mix gently but thoroughly, and stuff the turkey with it, closing the opening, of course, either with skewers, or sewing (I always put the heel of a loaf of bread over the opening, and then sew the skin together over it).

You may have your own favorite way of roasting the turkey. I prefer to use a low temperature, because it assures better flavor and appearance, less shrinkage, and less loss of juices, 325 degrees for 3½ to 4½ hours. A splendid idea is to dip cheesecloth in melted butter and drape it over the turkey so that it covers the entire bird. Then brush it with melted butter throughout the baking time.

To make a luscious gravy, skim off the fat and pour into a bowl. Put ¼ cup of drippings back into the pan, and blend in thoroughly the flour. Cook until bubbly, stirring constantly. Then add the water and dry white wine, and salt and pepper to taste. Cook, stirring constantly, until the gravy is thickened, about 5 minutes.

There are no doubt many people, who like myself, become a little taste-tired of the standard bread crumbs, sausage, and sage stuffing. So when a friend of mine sent me a recipe for a pecan and mushroom combination stuffing, I told the Little Woman that I would prepare and stuff the turkey, and she was delighted to get that job off her hands. When she tasted the finished product, her praise was heartwarming.

PECAN AND CORN BREAD STUFFING

Turkey giblets
3 cups crumbled cold corn bread
1 teaspoon nutmeg
4 tbsp. chopped parsley
½ tsp. thyme
½ tsp. marjoram
¼ tsp. ground mace
5 hard-cooked eggs

2 cups chopped pecan meats
4 oz. butter
1½ cups chopped mushrooms
1 large mild onion
½ cup chopped celery
Salt
Freshly ground pepper
⅔ cup sherry

Parboil the turkey giblets in enough salted water to cover.

To 3 cups of crumbled cold corn bread add 1 teaspoon of nutmeg, 4 tablespoons of chopped parsley, ½ teaspoon each of thyme and marjoram, ¼ teaspoon of ground mace, 2 cups of chopped pecan meats, and 5 hard-cooked eggs, chopped. Blend all these well.

Put 2 ounces of butter in a saucepan, and when hot add 1½ cups of coarsely chopped mushrooms, and the drained and chopped giblets. Sauté these for about 6 or 7 minutes.

In another saucepan put 2 ounces of butter, and when hot add 1 large mild onion, peeled and chopped, and ½ cup of chopped celery. When the onion is tender, mix with the mushrooms and giblets, and then transfer this mixture to the corn bread and pecan mixture. Season with salt and freshly ground pepper to taste, add about ⅔ cup of sherry, and blend well. The stuffing should just nicely hang together, but it should not be wet or pasty. Transfer the stuffing to the turkey, and roast in the usual way.

The following Thanksgiving, my much better half asked, a touch wistfully, whether I wanted to stuff the turkey again for Thanksgiving. She didn't know it, but I had stacked away the necessary ingredients for another terrific stuffing. This time it was a brandied chestnut stuffing.

BRANDIED CHESTNUT STUFFING

2 lb. chestnuts	1 tsp. chopped chives
1 cup cooking oil	½ tsp. thyme
2 cups consommé	½ tsp. marjoram
2 tbsp. butter	1 large bay leaf
6 little green onions	Salt
2 stalks celery	Pepper
¾ lb. sausage meat	2 cups soft bread crumbs
1 tbsp. chopped parsley	Madeira
½ cup brandy	

Pick over enough chestnuts to have 2 pounds of sound nuts. With a sharp and pointed knife cut an "X" on the flat side of the chestnuts. Heat 1 cup of cooking oil in a heavy skillet, and put in the chestnuts. Let them heat over a fast flame for about 3 minutes, shaking the pan and stirring the chestnuts all the while. Remove, drain, and the minute they can be handled, remove the shells and the inner skin. Put the shelled and skinned nuts into a saucepan with 2 cups of consommé, and let them cook until they are tender.

In a skillet melt 2 tablespoons of butter, and when the butter is hot add 6 little green onions (bulbs and tops), chopped, and 2 stalks of celery, chopped. When the onions begin to take on a little color add ¾ pound of sausage meat, 1 tablespoon of chopped parsley, 1 teaspoon of chopped chives, ½ teaspoon each of thyme and marjoram, and 1 large bay leaf, finely crumbled. Salt and pepper to taste, and sauté the whole for about 4 minutes, stirring constantly with a fork to break up the sausage meat and to blend the whole thoroughly.

Moisten 2 cups of soft bread crumbs with a little Madeira and add them, along with ½ cup of brandy, to the contents of the skillet. Mix well, and then add the chestnuts, which have been coarsely chopped. Again stir the mixture, and then stuff the turkey with it. Put the turkey in a roaster, adding a basting mixture of 1 cup of water and 1 cup of dry American white wine. Roast in a moderate oven (325-350 degrees) until the turkey is tender—about 15 to 20 minutes to the pound for 12- to 16-pound birds.

Nowadays, most of us "shoot" our turkeys off the counter of the market, while a lurking butcher leers at your pocketbook from behind his scales. But we can re-create at least the illusion of a wild turkey to a farm-raised bird with this wild rice stuffing, for it gives a suggestion of a wild turkey flavor.

WILD RICE STUFFING FOR TURKEY

2 cups raw wild rice
Tepid water
½ cup olive oil
1 cup finely diced celery
1 cup chopped onion
½ cup dry sherry wine
1 cup sliced fresh mushrooms
½ cup chopped green pepper

1 *can condensed beef*   1 *tbsp. chopped parsley*
  consommé   2 *tsp. salt*
        1 *tsp. Angostura bitters*

Wash the uncooked wild rice, and soak for an hour in
tepid water. Heat the olive oil in a heavy skillet and then,
stirring constantly, add the drained wild rice and the
finely diced celery and chopped onion. When blended, add
the condensed beef consommé and dry sherry. Then
stir in the sliced fresh mushrooms, chopped green pepper,
chopped parsley, salt, and Angostura bitters. Cover tightly, and allow to simmer for ½ hour, or until rice is done.

This dressing is best, and the flavor is improved, if the
mixture is cooled in a bowl and kept overnight in the refrigerator.

This Turkey à la King, which I will guarantee will be
different from any other you have ever tasted, can be
made in the morning, and reheated to serve in a casserole or chafing dish.

TURKEY À LA KING

3 *tbsp. butter*   4 *tbsp. cream*
2 *tbsp. flour*   3 *cups diced cooked turkey*
½ *small bay leaf*   3 *tbsp. butter*
½ *tsp. salt*   1 *cup chopped green pepper*
Pinch *freshly ground pepper* 1½ *cups sliced fresh mush-*
Dash *powdered nutmeg*   *rooms*
1 *cup rich milk*   3 *tbsp. chopped pimento*
¾ *cup mayonnaise*   3 *oz. dry Madeira wine*

Melt 3 tablespoons of butter in a saucepan over a medium flame. Then blend in the flour, the small bay leaf,
salt, a pinch of freshly ground pepper, and a dash of nutmeg. Remove the saucepan from the fire, and stir in
the rich milk very slowly. Return the saucepan to the heat
and stir constantly while cooking for about 10 minutes—
or until the sauce is thickened to the consistency of heavy
cream. Remove the saucepan from the heat, take out the
bay leaf, and gently mix in the mayonnaise, stirring con-

stantly. Then add the cream, and stir until the mixture is well blended. Next add the cooked, diced turkey meat. Incidentally, the foregoing recipe, up to the adding of the turkey, makes a superb rich cream sauce, or white sauce.

In a frying pan melt 3 tablespoons of butter, and in it lightly sauté the chopped green pepper and sliced fresh mushrooms until tender—about 10 minutes. Then add these to the cream sauce and turkey, and let simmer gently over a low flame for about 10 minutes, stirring constantly. Remove from the heat and add the chopped pimento and dry Madeira wine (if you haven't the Madeira, use 2 ounces of sweet [cream] sherry and 1 ounce of dry sherry). Blend well, and serve. If you make this ahead for serving later, be sure to let the mixture cool thoroughly without a cover until time to reheat. The recipe serves 6 generously.

VEGETABLES, 9. POTATOES, AND RICE

There is scarcely anything more tempting to the eye and appetite than the natural colors and flavors of fresh vegetables, or even the frozen vegetables. A properly prepared vegetable dish can raise the finest meal to undreamed-of heights, but vegetables served after a long exposure to a swimming pool of cooking water can ruin the efforts of the most expert chef.

The possible combinations of wines and vegetables, or sauces and vegetables, are almost endless, and would fill a fair-sized book. Such combinations offer a fertile field for the adventuresome and imaginative cook.

Mushrooms marry beautifully with a number of comestibles, but they mate succulently with string beans. Try the following combination at your next dinner party, and I can assure you that it will rate raves.

STRING BEANS WITH MUSHROOM SAUCE

1 lb. fresh mushrooms
2½ oz. butter
1 tsp. salt
1 lb. fresh string beans

1 tbsp. flour
3 oz. dry Madeira wine
2 cups cream

Slightly salted water
½ tsp. granulated sugar
Pinch dried savory

In a saucepan sauté the fresh mushrooms, sliced thin, in 1½ ounces of butter until the mushrooms are tender —about 8 to 10 minutes. Then sprinkle in the flour, blending it with the butter in the pan. Then blend in the dry Madeira (sercial). Next add the cream and ½ teaspoon of salt. Stir over a low flame until smooth and thickened, and keep hot.

Cook the small green string beans in slightly salted water for about 10 to 15 minutes, or until tender. (Frozen string beans can be used, and if so, follow directions on the package for cooking.) Drain off the water, add ½ teaspoon of salt, the fine granulated sugar, a pinch of savory, and 1 ounce of butter. Stir over a very low flame to heat thoroughly.

Place the string beans in the center of a dish, and pour the mushroom sauce around them.

Broccoli is really a very delicious vegetable, but it is usually subjected to mighty rough treatment in many kitchens. Too often, boiled for a long time, it comes out wilted and a muddy green color, and practically unfit for human consumption.

Broccoli can well be cooked as asparagus is cooked —in the bottom of a double boiler with the top inverted over it. I like it served with melted butter, or Hollandaise sauce, but it is at its delectable best served with an almond sauce.

BROCCOLI, ALMOND SAUCE

3 10-oz. pkgs. frozen broc-
    coli spears
3 egg yolks
1 tsp. cornstarch
½ cup dry white wine

1 tbsp. lemon juice
¼ cup melted butter
¼ tsp. Ac'cent.
Salt
Cayenne pepper

½ cup slivered almonds

Cook the broccoli according to directions on the package. Beat the egg yolks slightly in the top of a double boiler, then blend in the cornstarch, and add the dry white wine, lemon juice, and melted butter. Cook over boiling water in the bottom of the double boiler, stirring constantly for 2 or 3 minutes, or until thickened. Add the Ac'cent, salt and cayenne pepper to taste, and the slivered almonds. When heated, pour the sauce over the cooked broccoli. This serves 6.

Tender baby carrots are particularly delicious. One evening I was in an experimental mood. I had had a sidecar cocktail, which I'm very fond of, so I concocted a glaze for baby carrots in which the ingredients for a sidecar are a base, and this is what resulted.

CARROTS À LA SIDECAR

24 *baby carrots*	3 *oz. lemon juice*
Butter	2 *oz. brandy*
1 *oz. Cointreau*	2 *oz. honey*
	Parsley

Put about 24 baby carrots in cold, salted water, bring to a boil, and cook until just tender, about 15 minutes. Then remove them from the water, drain, and lay in a single layer in a buttered baking dish.

Make a syrup of the Cointreau, lemon juice, brandy, and honey. Pour this over the carrots and bake in a moderate oven (350 degrees) for about 15 minutes, basting occasionally with the syrup.

Sprinkle with parsley, and serve.

As a vegetable, the lowly onion was, for a great many years, favored only by those who lived "on the wrong side of the tracks." But through the ingenuity of many chefs, they have become a gourmet dish. Take, for instance, smothered onions with black walnuts and sherry!

GOURMET ONIONS

3 *dozen small onions*	*Flour*
Condensed consommé	1/3 *cup butter*
Dry sherry wine	1 *cup broken black walnuts*

Wash and peel the onions, put them in a heatproof baking dish, cover them halfway with equal parts of condensed consommé and dry sherry, cover, and bake in a 350-degree oven for ½ hour. Then uncover, turn the onions, dredge them with flour, add the butter, and sprinkle over them the broken-up black walnuts. Recover, and continue baking for about 15 minutes, or until the onions are tender.

French housewives combine peas and lettuce in a dish called Green Peas *bonne Femme,* which means "housewife style." It is at its best using fresh peas.

GREEN PEAS BONNE FEMME

4 *lbs. fresh peas*	6 *oz. condensed consommé*
1 *head romaine lettuce*	6 *oz. dry white wine*
3 *tbsp. butter*	*Pinch dried marjoram*
2 *slices bacon*	1 *tbsp. chopped parsley*
12 *little green onions*	1 *tbsp. chopped celery*
1 *tbsp. flour*	*leaves*
	Salt and pepper

Shell 4 pounds of peas and cut a head of romaine lettuce into shreds. In a casserole melt the butter and lightly brown in it the thin slices of bacon and sliced little green onions (bulbs only). Then add the flour, and blend well until smooth, and the lettuce. Pour into the casserole the canned condensed consommé and dry white wine, bring to a boil, stirring constantly. Let it simmer for a few minutes, then add a pinch of dried marjoram, the chopped parsley and chopped celery leaves, and the shelled peas. Salt and pepper to taste, and cook gently for about ½ hour, stirring frequently. Serve from the casserole.

Maybe spinach *suprème* isn't a dish you'd think of serving to Junior, but anyone with a true appreciation of delicious flavors will love it.

SPINACH SUPRÈME

2 *lb. fresh spinach*	1 *tsp. Worcestershire sauce*
4 *tbsp. butter*	*Freshly ground pepper*
1 *tsp. lime juice*	½ *cup sour cream*
Salt	¼ *lb. fresh mushrooms*
	¼ *cup Madeira wine*

Wash 2 pounds of fresh spinach quickly in warm water (not hot) to release any sand, then wash several times in cold water. Discard any wilted leaves. Put the washed spinach in about ½ cup of salted water, cover, and cook over a low heat for about 10 minutes, or until tender. Remove the spinach, and drain, then put it through the meat grinder, using the finest blade.

Put the chopped spinach in a saucepan with 2 tablespoons of butter, add 1 teaspoon of Worcestershire sauce, 1 teaspoon of lime juice, ½ cup of sour cream, and salt and freshly ground pepper to taste. Beat all this well together, and keep warm.

In a separate saucepan melt 2 tablespoons of butter, and sauté ¼ pound of fresh mushrooms, thinly sliced, for about 7 or 8 minutes. Then add the sautéed mushrooms to the spinach and sour cream, and add ¼ cup of Madeira. Mix all well, and simmer for 2 or 3 minutes over a medium flame. Serve at once.

One of the great Alsatian dishes is *Choucroute Alsacienne*. It was a specialty at the Alsatian Café in Paris, and a rare treat at several inns throughout Alsace. To me, it is sauerkraut raised to the nth degree of deliciousness.

CHOUCROUTE ALSACIENNE
(Sauerkraut)

2 *lb. sauerkraut*	6 *juniper berries*
1 *onion*	*Salt*
2 *carrots*	4 *thin slices smoked ham*
1 *large sweet apple*	*Butter*

| Lean bacon | 1 cup consommé |
| 10 peppercorns | 1 cup champagne |

Wash 2 pounds of sauerkraut in several changes of water and drain well, pressing to remove all water.

Chop 1 onion and 2 carrots fine and pare, core, and slice 1 large sweet apple.

Cover the bottom of an earthenware casserole with slices of lean bacon. Then add a layer of sauerkraut. Cover the sauerkraut with a layer of chopped onions, chopped carrots, and apple slices (about half the quantity of each), and sprinkle over the chopped vegetables about 10 bruised peppercorns and 6 bruised juniper berries, and salt lightly. Then add another thin layer of sauerkraut, and over that place 2 thin slices of smoked ham (Prosciutto ham is perfect). Next, comes a thin layer of sauerkraut, another layer of the chopped vegetables and apple slices, another thin layer of sauerkraut, 2 more slices of the thin ham, and a topping layer of the sauerkraut. Dot with butter, and pour over the contents of the casserole 1 cup of consommé and 1 cup of domestic champagne.

Cover the casserole tightly, and let cook slowly for about 4 hours. If more moistening is needed, add a little more champagne.

There is nothing that can beat properly prepared Boston Baked Beans, unless is is beans baked in the Brittany manner, or the way they bake frijole beans out in the great open spaces of the Southwest. However, at the risk of being banned in Boston, I'm going to give you an authentic Boston Baked Bean recipe with what I think is a slight improvement over the usual one.

BOSTON BAKED BEANS

1½ lb. navy beans	½ to ⅔ cup molasses
Bouquet garni:	¼ cup brown sugar
1 bay leaf	2 tsp. dry mustard
2 sprigs celery leaves	2 tsp. salt
10 sprigs fresh parsley	¼ tsp. pepper

| 1 *sprig thyme* | 1 *medium-sized onion* |
| 1/2 *lb. salt pork* | 1 *cup sherry* |

Pick over 1½ pounds of navy beans (or any other variety that you fancy), cover with cold water, and let soak overnight, or for 12 hours. Cover with additional water, into which a *bouquet garni* of 1 bay leaf, 2 sprigs of celery leaves, about 10 sprigs of fresh parsley, and a sprig of thyme has been put. Cook over a low heat until the skins break if you blow on them—about 1 to 1½ hours. Drain the beans, reserving the liquid. Slice ½ pound of salt pork in ¼-inch slices. Put the beans and half of the sliced pork, in alternate layers, in a 2-quart bean pot or casserole. Now score remainder of the pork slices, and put them on top of the beans in the center.

Next, mix ½ to ⅔ cup of molasses, ¼ cup of brown sugar, 2 teaspoons of dry mustard, 2 teaspoons of salt, ¼ teaspoon of pepper, and 1 minced medium-sized onion with 2 cups of the liquid you have drained off the beans, and pour the mixture over the beans. Cover and bake in a slow oven (250 degrees) for 6 to 8 hours. And now comes the *pièce de résistance*. One hour before the baking is finished, pour 1 cup of sherry over the beans, put the cover back on, and let bake the remaining hour.

Pommes de Terre Soufflées, or Balloon Potatoes, as they are sometimes called by the uninitiated, never fail to bring forth exclamations of delight whenever they are served. They seldom appear on the menus of any but the most exclusive restaurants, and they are seldom prepared in the home, because they are thought to be very difficult to cook so that the potatoes arrive at the table really looking like little oblong-shaped balloons.

There is really nothing mysterious about *Pommes de Terre Soufflées,* and they shouldn't be too hard to make. But certain precautions must be taken: New potatoes cannot be used, oldish potatoes of a mellow texture are best; the slices must be very thin, not over an eighth of an inch thick; and the fat they are cooked in must be of two different degrees of heat.

POMMES DE TERRE SOUFFLÉES

Peel the raw potatoes, and cut into slices not to exceed ⅛ inch in thickness. The slices must be of uniform size and thickness, trimmed to the shape of a flattened football. Put the slices in ice water for a few minutes, or run very cold water over them to remove any extra starch. Then they should be dried.

Heat a kettle of fat (lard is the best) to a temperature just below the boiling point, or just as it begins to smoke. Keep the full heat under the pot, as the cold potatoes cool the fat slightly. Let the slices cook until they begin to show a pale gold color, and the edges show faint signs of puffing. This should take about 3 minutes. Then remove the slices, drain them well in a collander or strainer, and allow to cool for about 5 minutes.

Most chefs insist upon 2 kettles of fat, the first one having a moderate temperature, just below boiling, and the other a high temperature, boiling and smoking. But it is possible to get by, I am told, with one pot of fat. After the initial immersion of the potatoes in the fat with a moderate temperature, turn the heat up and, while the potatoes are cooling, bring the fat to a boiling and smoking temperature.

When the potatoes have cooled, put a few slices at a time in the really hot fat, using a frying basket or a coarse sieve. It will probably be necessary to experiment with one or two before you learn the moment when they should be removed. This second frying is very quick, a matter of seconds rather than minutes. The potatoes should be properly crisp and brown, but not burned, when they are taken out. Drain them on absorbent paper, sprinkle with salt, and serve very hot.

Some night, when you have leftover boiled potatoes, or leftover browned potatoes which have been cooked with a roast, try sherried potatoes with mushrooms. This is a simple yet savory dish, adaptable to whatever number of people you want to serve. I am purposely leaving out the amount of ingredients, because you can measure them according to your needs.

SHERRIED POTATOES WITH MUSHROOMS

Sliced cooked potatoes   *Salt and pepper*
Condensed cream of mush-   *Dry sherry*
     room soup   *Fine bread crumbs*
          Grated Parmesan cheese

Place a layer of sliced cooked potatoes in the bottom of a casserole, salt and pepper them to taste, and cover with condensed cream of mushroom soup. Then add another layer of the sliced cooked potatoes, salt and pepper them, and add another layer of the cream of mushroom soup. Continue layers until the casserole is nearly full. Then sprinkle over the contents of the casserole some dry sherry wine, cover the top with fine bread-crumbs, sprinkle with grated Parmesan cheese, and bake in a moderate (350 degrees) oven until hot.

Sweet potatoes are of two types: one has pale yellow flesh, which cooks dry and mealy; and the other has a deeper orange flesh, which is sweeter and more moist. The latter is called a yam commercially, although it isn't actually a yam. The true yam is a native of Africa. Sweet potatoes seem to lend themselves to more exotic preparation than the white, or Irish potato. This dish can well be the *pièce de résistance* at any dinner, and it seems to go best with pork dishes.

SWEET POTATOES IN SHELLS

6 sweet potatoes   *2 oz. butter*
Bacon fat   *Pinch freshly ground pepper*
3 oz. rum   *1 tsp. salt*
3 oz. brandy   *Powdered cinnamon*

Wash 6 medium to large sweet potatoes, rub their skins with bacon fat, and bake in a hot oven (450 degrees) until tender—about 40 minutes.

Cut each potato in half, lengthwise, and remove the pulp, being careful not to break the shells.

Mash the potato pulp, then add 3 ounces of rum, 3 ounces of brandy, 2 ounces of butter, 1 teaspoon of salt, and a pinch of freshly ground pepper. Whip this mixture until it is smooth and fluffy, and put it back in the sweet potato shells. Sprinkle the tops with a little cinnamon, and place in the oven to brown.

On Italian freighters, spaghetti is a staple food. Because ships' stores always contain olive oil, garlic, canned tomatoes, onions, and tinned anchovies, a favorite sailor dish is Spaghetti Marinara.

SPAGHETTI MARINARA

8 *oz. spaghetti*	1 *large can tomatoes*
3 *qt. boiling water*	10 *canned anchovy fillets,*
1 *tbsp. salt*	*chopped*
4 *tbsp. Olive Oil*	2 *oz. dry white wine*
2 *cloves garlic*	*Freshly ground pepper*
2 *medium-sized onions*	¼ *tsp. dried oregano*
Grated Parmesan cheese	

Add the salt to the rapidly boiling water, and then gradually add the spaghetti so that the water continues to boil. Cook, uncovered, until tender, about 10 to 12 minutes.

Put the olive oil in a heavy saucepan, and when it is hot add the garlic, crushed, and the onions, sliced. Sauté for 5 to 10 minutes, or until the onions are soft. Then add the tomatoes, and cook rapidly for about 5 minutes. Add the chopped anchovy fillets, the dry white wine, freshly ground pepper, and the dried oregano. Lower the flame, and simmer for about 45 minutes.

Drain the spaghetti, and pour the sauce over it. Sprinkle with grated Parmesan cheese, and serve immediately. This will serve 3.

One of the great Italian *pasta* dishes, usually served in a baking dish, is *lasagne*. It is named after the Italian broad noodles. Here is the recipe for Lasagne, which I think is pretty fine.

LASAGNE

1 *lb. ground chuck beef*	1 *pkg. Lawry's Spaghetti*
2 *tbsp. olive oil*	*Sauce Mix*
2 *cloves garlic, minced*	½ *lb. lasagne*
Seasoned salt	*Salted water*
Pepper	½ *lb. mozzarella cheese*
1 *8-oz. can tomato paste*	½ *cup grated Parmesan*
1 *#2 can tomatoes*	*cheese*

¾ *lb. ricotta cheese*

Brown the ground chuck beef in the olive oil in a large skillet, adding the minced garlic to the beef, and seasoned salt, and pepper to taste. Simmer slowly for about 10 minutes. Then add the tomato sauce or paste, the canned tomatoes, and the package of spaghetti sauce mix. Stir everything thoroughly, cover, and simmer for 30 minutes.

Meanwhile, boil ½ pound of lasagne in salted water until tender (about 20 to 25 minutes) stirring frequently to prevent the lasagne sticking together. When just barely tender, drain the lasagne well, and rinse.

Arrange a layer of the meat sauce in the bottom of a large casserole. Cover this with a layer of lasagne. Then make a layer of mozzarella cheese (a soft Italian cheese, usually sold in balls at Italian grocery stores) over the lasagne. Dot the slices of mozzarella cheese with ricotta cheese (an Italian cottage cheese). Repeat the layers, ending up with a layer of lasagne and sauce. Sprinkle generously with grated Parmesan cheese, and bake in a 375-degree oven for about 20 minutes. The total amounts of the cheeses needed are ½ pound of mozzarella, ¾ pound of ricotta, and ½ cup of Parmesan, grated. This recipe will serve about 6. Of course, an Italian-type wine, such as Barbera or Chianti, is a must.

The best *Risotto Milanaise* I've ever eaten is that which is prepared by a captain in Riccardo's Restaurant in Chicago, Alex Pucci. If you'll follow the directions, I know you can turn out this delicious dish.

RISOTTO MILANAISE À LA PUCCI

1½ cups uncooked long-grain rice
¼ lb. butter
1 large Bermuda onion
½ lb. diced Italian ham
3 oz. dry white wine
4¼ cups chicken broth
¼ tsp. powdered saffron
Salt
Pepper
¼ cup chopped mushrooms
Pinch nutmeg
½ cup grated Parmesan cheese

In a large heavy iron skillet melt ¼ pound of butter. When it is hot, but not brown, add 1 large Bermuda onion, peeled and chopped fine, and ½ pound of diced Italian ham (again, Prosciutto ham is the best, but ordinary ham will do). Sauté the onion and ham gently for about 10 minutes. Then add 1½ cups of long-grain rice, which has previously been thoroughly washed in cold running water and later completely dried. Stir constantly with a wooden fork until the rice begins to brown, which should be about 20 minutes. Then add 3 ounces of dry California white wine. Still stirring the rice, let it absorb the wine, which will take about 2 minutes. Then add 4 cups of boiling hot chicken broth, a little salt and pepper, a tiny pinch of nutmeg, and ¼ cup of chopped fresh mushrooms. Stir thoroughly with a wooden fork or spoon, then cover, and let simmer over a very low flame for about 20 minutes.

Dissolve ¼ teaspoon of powdered saffron in ¼ cup of hot chicken broth. Add this to the rice, along with ½ cup of grated Parmesan cheese. Stir gently but thoroughly, and cook for 10 minutes more. Remove from the fire, let stand for a couple of minutes, and serve.

There seems to be a bit of confusion in the minds of a large number of people about wild rice. Many believe that wild rice is just what its name might imply—ordinary rice that grows wild, or is not cultivated. But, as a matter of fact, wild rice is not a true cereal, as rice is, but is the seed of a tall, broad aquatic grass, native to North America. It is found in fresh water and brackish swamps, in nearly all states east of the Rocky Mountains.

WILD RICE WITH MUSHROOM SAUCE

2 cups wild rice	1 cup chopped onion
3 qt. boiling water	1 tsp. salt
½ lb. bacon	½ tsp. pepper
½ cup butter	1 cup chicken broth
1 cup chopped celery	2 cans cream of mush-
½ cup chopped green	room soup
pepper	1 can mushrooms

Soak the wild rice in warm water for 2 hours, washing it several times, and then drain. In a large saucepan, have 3 quarts of water boiling vigorously. Add the wild rice, and when the water boils again, turn off the heat, and let it stand, covered, for 10 minutes. Then drain it again. During this time chop the bacon and fry until crisp.

In a skillet or saucepan put in the butter, and when it is hot add the chopped celery, chopped onion, and the seeded, chopped green pepper, the salt and pepper. Sauté until celery, green pepper, and onion are about half done. Then mix the rice, the bacon, the sautéed celery, onion, and green pepper, and the chicken broth, place in a greased baking dish, cover, and let bake in a 375-degree oven for ½ hour. While this is baking, mix together the cream of mushroom soup and a can of mushrooms with their juice, and heat thoroughly. Serve the rice with the mushroom sauce poured over it.

Bulghour is processed from wheat, and, to my way of thinking, is far superior to rice. It is cooked in the same way, but has much more taste. It can be obtained in any Armenian or Greek store.

BULGHOUR

| 2 tbsp. butter | 1 cup Bulghour |
| 1 small onion, chopped | 2 cups chicken broth |

You merely melt the butter in a heavy kettle, and add the small onion, chopped very fine. Simmer the onion for a few minutes (be careful not to brown the onion) and then add the *Bulghour*. Stir and mix, and then add the boiling chicken broth. Mix well with a wooden spoon, and bring to a fast boil. Then cover tightly, reduce the flame to the lowest possible point, and let simmer for 20 minutes. The liquid should be entirely absorbed. This serves 4 people.

Bulghour goes with practically any meat dish, but it is particularly delicious with lamb.

There is no more perfect accompaniment to roast beef than Yorkshire pudding. Yet it is almost impossible to find a light and delicious Yorkshire pudding in restaurants and the majority of homes. What one usually encounters is as tough as shoe leather, or a soggy mess that is repulsive. However, here is a recipe that is easy to make, and the method is foolproof. It comes out crisp and brown, like popovers, and with absolutely no sogginess.

YORKSHIRE PUDDING

1½ cups sifted flour	1 tsp. nutmeg
1 tsp. salt	4 eggs
1 tsp. pepper	1½ cups scalded milk
½ cup beef fat drippings	

Mix together the flour, salt, pepper, and nutmeg (don't be alarmed at the amount of pepper). To this add the beaten eggs (one at a time) and the milk, added little by little. Stir well and beat again with a rotary beater. Cover with a cloth and chill in refrigerator for at least 2 hours.

When the roast is done and taken out of the oven, put ½ cup of drippings into a shallow pan, and set pan in oven to become sizzling hot. Then beat the chilled batter vigorously, and pour it into the pan of hot fat. It should be about ½ inch deep in the pan. Bake in a 450-degree oven for about 15 minutes, or until pudding has risen. Then reduce heat to 300 degrees, and bake 15 minutes longer, or until pudding is crisp and brown. To serve, cut pudding in squares, and place around the roast on the platter.

SALADS, SALAD 10. DRESSINGS, AND SAUCES

The rules for making an acceptable salad are few and simple. The ingredients should be strictly fresh, thoroughly chilled, and absolutely dry. The dressing, which is the final touch contributing to a salad's perfection, should be carefully compounded. Harsh vinegars are to be avoided, and only the finest olive oil should be used.

One of the outstanding salads, in my opinion, is a Caesar Salad. It serves admirably as a first-course salad, or a separate course salad.

CAESAR SALAD

6 *slices French bread*	½ *tsp. salt*
10 *tbsp. olive oil*	1 *tsp. dry mustard*
4 *cloves garlic*	1 *tsp. freshly ground*
1 *tsp. salt*	*pepper*
2 *tbsp. red wine vinegar*	4 *fillets anchovies*

1 tbsp. fresh lemon juice
½ tsp. Worcestershire
    sauce

1 tbsp. grated Parmesan
    cheese
1 lb. romaine lettuce
1 raw egg

First, prepare the croutons, which can (and should be) fixed hours in advance. Cut 6 slices of French (or Italian) bread ½ inch thick, and then cut each slice into 6 pieces. In a heavy skillet put about 4 tablespoons of olive oil and 2 small cloves of garlic which have been cut in slivers. When the oil is hot, add the pieces of bread, and sauté until they are golden brown on all sides. Then set them aside until ready to use.

In a large wooden salad bowl place 2 medium-sized cloves of garlic which have been cut in half, and sprinkle them with 1 teaspoon of salt. Crush the cloves of garlic with a fork, mixing the crushed cloves and salt around in the bowl. This takes about 2 minutes. If you are very fond of garlic, leave the crushed pieces and the salt in the bowl. Or, if you prefer, discard both the garlic and the salt.

Put 6 tablespoons of the best olive oil (I like Old Monk brand) in the salad bowl and beat with a fork for about 1 minute, or until thick. Then add 2 tablespoons of red wine vinegar (I make bold to recommend the Spice Islands vinegars) and 1 tablespoon of fresh lemon juice, and beat well with the fork until thoroughly blended with the olive oil. Next add the Worcestershire sauce, the dry mustard, ½ teaspoon of salt, the freshly ground pepper, the fillets of anchovies cut into small pieces, and the grated Parmesan cheese. Again beat the whole with the fork until well blended.

Now add the romaine lettuce, which has been washed, thoroughly dried, and well chilled, and broken into medium-sized pieces. Toss well with a wooden salad fork and spoon until the lettuce pieces are well marinated, but not so vigorously as to bruise the lettuce. Next add a whole raw egg (if you desire, you can coddle the egg by placing it in a bowl of very hot water for 5 minutes) broken over the lettuce, and again mix well, but gently. Last, add the croutons (which have been previously sautéed) and toss with the salad. However, don't toss so much that the croutons become soggy. They should be crisp and crunchy. Serve the salads at once on salad plates or in wooden salad bowls.

This was the favorite salad of the late Edgar Guest, and it is superb.

MY SALAD

1½ cups cooked chicken
3 cups shredded lettuce
1 cup mayonnaise dressing
1 tbsp. tarragon vinegar
2 tbsp. chili sauce
1 tbsp. chopped green pepper
1 tbsp. chopped pimento
6 ounces Roquefort (or blue) cheese
Lettuce leaves

Mix 1½ cups of chicken (or turkey) cut in julienne strips with 3 cups of shredded lettuce.

To 1 cup of thick mayonnaise dressing add 1 tablespoon of tarragon vinegar, 2 tablespoons of chili sauce, 1 tablespoon of chopped green pepper, 1 tablespoon of chopped pimento, and 6 ounces of Rouquefort (or blue) cheese, crumbled. Blend well.

Add this dressing to the chicken and lettuce, mix gently, and place the whole mixture in a bowl lined with lettuce leaves.

An unusual potato salad is this one that combines meat, potatoes, and vegetables into one delicious dish—an ideal main dish for a hot night.

POTATO SALAD DE LUXE

½ cup chopped celery
6 tbsp. olive oil
4 tsp. fresh lemon juice
¼ cup minced onion
1 tsp. salt
⅛ tsp. pepper
2 cups sliced cooked potatoes
1½ cups sliced mushrooms
¼ cup shredded raw carrots
2 cups diced cooked meat (ham, chicken, tongue, lamb, beef)
Crisp lettuce
French or mayonnaise dressing

Sauté the sliced fresh mushrooms in the olive oil until tender. Let cool slightly, then add the fresh lemon juice, minced onion, salt, and pepper. Let stand until cold. Combine the sliced cooked potatoes, shredded raw carrots, chopped celery, diced cooked tongue (or ham, chicken, beef, or lamb). Pour mushroom mixture over all and marinate at least 1 hour. Serve on a bed of crisp lettuce. A French or mayonnaise dressing may be served if desired.

Coleslaw goes perfectly with broiled fish or spareribs. As far as I am concerned, it is a must. So what have I done? I've devised a coleslaw of my own, and I do think it is damn good.

PIQUANT COLESLAW

1 head cabbage
Ice water
⅓ cup tarragon white wine
     vinegar
2 tbsp. sugar
½ tsp. salt
¼ tsp. pepper
Paprika
½ cup chopped green
     pepper

2 tbsp. chopped pimiento
1 tbsp. chopped little green
     onions
¼ tsp. celery seed
¼ tsp. dried dill weed
¼ tsp. caraway seeds
½ cup mayonnaise
½ cup sour cream
1 tbsp. horseradish

Shred the cabbage, and then soak in ice water for about 30 minutes. Drain, and dry thoroughly.

To the shredded cabbage add the white wine tarragon vinegar, sugar, salt, pepper, and a sprinkling of paprika. Toss and let marinate for 1 hour. Then drain (reserving the liquid) and lightly squeeze the cabbage to remove any excess liquid.

Add to the cabbage the green pepper, chopped pimiento, little green onions, celery seed, dried dill weed, and caraway seed. Again toss lightly.

Mix together the mayonnaise, sour cream, horseradish, and the reserved seasoned vinegar. Pour over the cabbage mixture, and toss lightly.

The Palace Hotel in San Francisco has become famous for the following dressing, which is indeed wonderful.

GREEN GODDESS DRESSING

To 1 cup of basic mayonnaise dressing add:

3 tbsp. finely chopped anchovies

3 tbsp. chopped chives (or little green onions)

1 clove garlic, grated

½ cup heavy cream

1 tbsp. lemon juice

3 tbsp. tarragon wine vinegar

⅛ cup chopped parsley

Salt

Freshly ground pepper

Put the above ingredients in an electric blender for 20 seconds, chill, and pour over mixed greens. This dressing is wonderful over limestone or Bibb lettuce. The Palace Hotel adds small cooked shrimps.

Many recipes for red wine French dressings call for catsup as an ingredient, but for myself I violently object to them. Catsup contains pungent spices, and it certainly tends to mask any delicate wine and herb flavors in the dressing. So I give you my version. (If you like your dressing with more olive oil in it, govern yourself accordingly.)

RED WINE DRESSING À LA WOOD

5 oz. olive oil

1 oz. red wine vinegar

2 oz. dry red wine

½ tsp. mustard

1 tsp. salt

Freshly ground pepper

½ tsp. Worcestershire sauce

Pinch basil

Pinch tarragon

1 tsp. sugar

Into an earthenware bowl put 5 ounces of pure olive oil, 1 ounce of red wine vinegar, 2 ounces of dry California red wine, ½ teaspoon of dry mustard, 1 teaspoon of salt, freshly ground pepper to taste, ½ teaspoon of Worcestershire sauce, a pinch each of basil and tarragon, and 1 teaspoon of sugar. Stir this until everything is well blended, and then set bowl in a container of ice to chill.

Knowing the hazards of making a Hollandaise sauce, I decided I would experiment, and see if I could devise a foolproof Hollandaise. I worked with a mayonnaise, and finally came up with something that is simple, easy, and very delicious.

MOCK HOLLANDAISE SAUCE

1 *cup mayonnaise*	2 *tbsp. lemon juice*
2 *generous tbsp. butter*	¼ *tsp. salt*
	¼ *tsp. paprika*

In a double boiler, over hot (not boiling) water, let the mayonnaise become well warmed. Then add the butter, broken into small pieces, and stir with a wire whisk, or table fork, constantly until the butter is melted. Then add the lemon juice and the seasonings, and stir until all is well blended.

The beauty of this sauce is that it can be made ahead, kept refrigerated, and rewarmed just before serving. Use it wherever Hollandaise sauce is called for.

A sauce I developed is called White Sauce Élégante. It is a super-rich cream sauce, and is very elegant.

WHITE SAUCE ÉLÉGANTE

2 *tbsp. butter*	1 *cup warm milk*
2 *tbsp. flour*	* ¾ *cup mayonnaise*
5 *peppercorns*	4 *tbsp. cream*
½ *tsp. salt*	1 *tbsp. butter*
½ *small bay leaf*	*Pinch ground nutmeg*

Melt 2 tablespoons of butter in a saucepan. Add the peppercorns (or a pinch of ground pepper), the salt, the grated nutmeg, the bay leaf, crumbled, and the flour. Cook over a medium flame, blending butter and flour until perfectly smooth (about 3 or 4 minutes, stirring constantly). Then add the warm milk very slowly, stirring constantly with a wire whisk, or spoon. Cook slowly, stirring frequently, for about 10 minutes, or until the sauce is thickened to the consistency of heavy cream.

Strain the sauce into another saucepan, and add to it the ¾ cup of mayonnaise (* add 1 cup if the finished sauce is to be refrigerated for 4 hours or more before using), stirring constantly. When the mayonnaise is well blended in, add the cream, and 1 pat of butter (about 1 tablespoon), and stir the whole until well blended. If a thinner sauce is desired, stir in additional cream.

This recipe makes about 1 pint of sauce. It is at its delicate best if refrigerated for 4 hours or more, and then gently reheated.

One of the things I am fondest of is spaghetti—"express" spaghetti, cooked *al dente* (to your individual order); Plain (*al burro*) with Parmesan cheese sprinkled over it; sailor style (*marinara*), or with a rich meat sauce is, in my opinion, a food for the gods.

This recipe for a meat sauce is rich, savory, and delectable. It is a combination of the recipe of a marvelous Italian cook and one devised by the late Crosby Gaige.

SPAGHETTI MEAT SAUCE DE LUXE

¼ cup butter	½ #2 can tomatoes
1 tbsp. olive oil	½ tbsp. Worcestershire
½ lb. ground chuck beef	sauce
½ lb. ground pork	½ tbsp. Angostura bitters
½ lb. ground veal	½ tbsp. sugar
½ green pepper, chopped	½ cup dry red wine
4 cloves garlic, minced	Salt
1 large onion	Pepper
½ lb. fresh mushrooms,	½ tsp. celery salt
chopped	2 bay leaves
1½ cans tomato paste	Dash cayenne pepper

In a large kettle heat ¼ cup of butter and 1 tablespoon of olive oil, and in this brown ½ pound each of ground chuck beef, ground pork, and ground veal. Then add ½ green pepper, chopped, 4 cloves of garlic, minced, 1 large onion, chopped, ½ pound of fresh mushrooms, chopped, 1½ cans of tomato paste (get this at an Italian grocery), ½ large can of tomatoes, ½ tablespoon of Worcestershire sauce, ½ tablespoon of Angostura bitters, ½ tablespoon of sugar, ½ cup of good dry California red wine (Chianti type), salt and pepper to taste, ½ teaspoon of celery salt, 2 crumbled bay leaves, and a generous dash of cayenne pepper. Cover this nectar, and cook very slowly for at least 3 hours.

There are almost as many versions of barbecue sauce as there are barbecues. But the finest, and most intriguing barbecue sauce I have ever tasted was devised by Ken Churchill, one of the top music arrangers in this country.

BARBECUE SAUCE

2 lb. onions	1 tsp. garlic salt
6 large cloves garlic	1 tbsp. oregano
½ cup bacon fat	2½ tbsp. paprika
½ cup catsup	½ tsp. red pepper
½ cup chili sauce	¼ tsp. marjoram
10 oz. tomato purée	1½ oz. chili powder
28 oz. tomatoes	1½ tsp. salt
12 oz. tomato juice	3 bay leaves
½ cup light vinegar	2 tsp. celery salt
½ cup dark vinegar	2 tsp. onion salt
¼ cup rum	1 tbsp. brown sugar
2 tbsp. Beau Monde	6 dashes Tabasco
seasoning	½ tsp. ground cloves

Brown 2 pounds of onions, finely chopped, and 6 large cloves of garlic, minced, in ½ cup of bacon fat. Then add the rest of the ingredients, mixing well.

EGGS
11. AND
CHEESE

I don't know of any comestible that can be as varied as eggs. While there are nine basic ways to cook eggs (soft-boiled, hard-cooked, fried, broiled, baked, poached, scrambled, and in omelets and in soufflés), I'd be willing to wager that I could serve eggs three hundred and sixty-five days running, and have a different dish every day.

Of all the recipes I have, the one most people frequently ask for is what I call Eggs Parmesan. It is the perfect breakfast dish. But don't serve it with bacon or sausage, but just with toast or muffins, so that alien flavors will not detract from its deliciousness.

EGGS PARMESAN

2 *eggs*
2 *tbsp. butter*
1 *oz. dry sherry*
Salt
2 *tbsp. grated Parmesan*
   cheese
Freshly ground pepper

Lightly brown 2 tablespoons of butter in a skillet, and as the butter takes on color, add 1 ounce of sherry. When the liquid begins to bubble, break 2 eggs into it. As the white begins to set, remove the skillet from the fire and sprinkle 2 tablespoons of grated Parmesan cheese over the eggs, after having seasoned them to taste with salt and freshly ground pepper.

Put the skillet under the broiler, and when the whites set and the cheese begins to brown, remove and serve. But watch the eggs carefully while they are under the broiler. The yolks should not be allowed to become hard, nor the cheese to burn.

Now, let's meet our friend, the egg, in the midst of black patent leather boots, red coats, dogs straining on the leash, eager horses, and "Tantivy!" At a hunt breakfast, this is the perfect dish.

SCRAMBLED EGGS À LA CHASSEUR

4 eggs	1 tsp. chopped chives
4 chicken livers	Salt
4 oz. butter	Pepper
8 mushrooms	1 tbsp. flour
1 little green onion	3 oz. consommé
1 tbsp. chopped parsley	3 tbsp. Madeira

Rinse 4 chicken livers in cold water, dry, and cut each one into quarters.

Melt 2 ounces of butter in a saucepan, and when hot add the chicken livers. Sauté gently for about 4 minutes, stirring frequently, then add 8 mushrooms, coarsely chopped, 1 little green onion (bulb and top), chopped, 1 tablespoon of chopped parsley, 1 teaspoon of chopped chives, salt and pepper, freshly ground, to taste, and sprinkle in 1 tablespoon of flour. Blend all these ingredients well, then add 3 ounces of consommé and 3 tablespoons of Madeira. Cover, and let simmer very gently for about 15 minutes.

Scramble 4 eggs lightly in 2 ounces of butter. Put

them on a hot platter, pour the sauce over, and serve hot.

Two of my favorite comestibles with eggs are chicken livers and mushrooms. I like to use them in scrambled eggs, and mushrooms go beautifully with this baked egg dish, which is perfect for a Sunday brunch. Let's be fancy and give it its French name.

OEUFS AUX CHAMPIGNONS
(Eggs with Mushrooms)

6 eggs
3 tbsp. butter
½ lb. fresh mushrooms
2 tbsp. flour
1 cup dry white wine
1 cup chicken broth

3 tbsp. mayonnaise
1 little green onion, chopped
1 tbsp. chopped parsley
Salt
Freshly ground pepper
2 tbsp. melted butter

Grated Gruyère cheese

Sauté the sliced fresh mushrooms in the butter in a saucepan. When they are lightly browned (about 8 minutes), stir in the flour, and blend well. Then add the dry white wine, chicken broth, mayonnaise, the chopped little green onion (bulb and top), and the chopped parsley. Season to taste with salt and freshly ground pepper, and cook, stirring, until the sauce is smooth.

Pour the sauce in a shallow baking dish, distributing it evenly. Then, carefully break the eggs over the sauce, distributing them evenly. Pour over all the melted butter, and sprinkle generously with the grated Gruyère (Parmesan can be used) cheese. Bake in a 350-degree oven until eggs are cooked. This will serve 3 or 6, depending upon how many eggs per person.

Another very delightful brunch dish is Devonshire Eggs, which is an old English dish, and brings back an old use of mint.

DEVONSHIRE EGGS

½ tsp. chopped fresh mint   1 tbsp. butter

½ cup dry white wine   1 tbsp. flour
½ tbsp. chopped little green   Salt
   onions   Pepper
1 tbsp. chopped parsley   1 tbsp. lemon juice
3 tbsp. fine bread crumbs   4 very fresh eggs
2 tbsp. grated Parmesan cheese   Butter

In a saucepan simmer the chopped fresh mint, little green onions, parsley, and the dry white wine for 15 minutes. At the end of the simmering time stir into the mixture a *roux* made with the tablespoon of butter and the flour creamed together, adding salt and pepper to taste and the lemon juice. Stir and blend until the sauce is smooth. If it becomes too thick, add a little more dry white wine.

Boil the *very fresh* eggs in water for 4 minutes. Remove from the water quickly, and let them cool in cool water. Then remove the shells (very carefully, lest the eggs break and spoil the dish) and lay the whole eggs in a shallow baking dish. Pour the sauce over them, and sprinkle with the bread crumbs which have been lightly sautéed in a little butter, and the grated Parmesan cheese. Heat the whole well in a 325-degree oven, and serve.

Omelets, in our house, are usually reserved for Sunday-morning breakfast which, to my mind, is one of the most delightful meals of the week. The type of omelet served varies with our moods. An *Omelet aux Fines Herbes* is delicately delicious. It is simple—you merely add ¼ teaspoon of dried *fines herbes* to the egg mixture before beating (*fines herbes* consists of a mixture of thyme, oregano, sage, rosemary, marjoram, and basil; these are in dried form, and can be purchased in bottled form in fine food shops and grocery stores).

I think our favorite omelet is a chicken liver omelet, and this is the way we make it.

CHICKEN LIVER OMELET

½ lb. chicken livers   1 tbsp. flour

Seasoned flour   ½ cup condensed consommé
3 tbsp. butter   ¼ cup dry Madeira wine
4 eggs   1 tsp. finely minced little
Butter   green onions
Salt   ¼ tsp. dried tarragon leaves
               Pepper

Clean the chicken livers and dredge them with seasoned flour. In a skillet put 2 tablespoons of butter, and when it is hot add the floured chicken livers and sauté them for about 7 minutes, or until their red-juiced look disappears and they are delicately colored on all sides. Then remove them to a hot dish and keep warm.

To the butter and juices in the skillet add another tablespoon of butter, the minced little green onions, and the dried tarragon. Sprinkle in 1 tablespoon of flour, and when well blended in stir in the condensed consommé and the dry Madeira wine. Simmer gently until the mixture thickens a little, then add the chicken livers, and let heat while making the omelet.

Prepare the omelet, using 4 eggs for 2 people. Remember, be generous with the butter (I use about 2 ounces) and heat it to bubbling in a heavy skillet. Pour in the well-beaten eggs, which have been seasoned with salt and pepper, and stir well until the eggs begin to set, then stop. When the eggs are done, but still a little moist on top, slide the omelet onto a hot platter, cover half of it with the chicken livers and sauce, fold the other half over, and pour the remaining chicken livers and sauce over, and serve. This is a generous serving for 2.

CHEESE

To my mind, the greatest cheese spread of all is Liptoi, a savory cheese from Hungary. It is perhaps better known by its German name, Liptauer.

Most recipes for this wonderful cheese omit two important ingredients, ale and mustard. The true Hungarian Liptoi is made from a cream cheese prepared from goat's milk, but a cream cheese will do very well.

LIPTOI CHEESE

½ lb. cream cheese
¼ cup sour cream
2 oz. softened butter
2 tsp. anchovy paste
2 tsp. drained capers

2 little green onions, chopped
⅛ tsp. salt
1 tbsp. paprika
2 tsp. caraway seeds
½ tsp. dry mustard
1 oz. ale

The best and easiest way to make Liptoi is in a blender. Into the detachable glass bowl of the blender put the cream cheese, broken up, the sour cream, the softened butter, the anchovy paste, the drained capers, the little green onions (shallots are even better if you can get them), the salt, the best paprika that you can obtain, the caraway seeds, the dry mustard, and the ale. Whip this mixture to a smooth blend. You may have to stop the blender a couple of times and stir the ingredients with a spatula, but when all is mixing well let the blender go until everything is smooth and creamy. Put the mixture into a bowl, and place in the refrigerator.

To serve, garnish with radishes, and accompany with thin slices of brown bread or pumpernickel. Dry sherry, chilled, or Dubonnet and dry vermouth, mixed half and half, and chilled, are the indicated libations.

Welsh rabbit is the classic chafing dish recipe, and to my mind, there is only one thing to make it with— stale ale or beer. My father was a master at making Welsh rabbit, and here's how he did it.

WELSH RABBIT

1 bottle stale ale
1 tbsp. butter
1 tbsp. dry mustard

1 lb. sharp American cheese
1 tbsp. Worcestershire sauce
Dash cayenne pepper
Dash paprika

In the morning my father opened a bottle of ale and

allowed it to stand all day; also, a pound of sharp American cheese was cut into small dice. Then, at night, when the guests were seated round the table after a game of five hundred or whist, the spirit lamp under the chafing dish was lighted, and a tablespoon of butter was melted in the pan. Next, the cheese was added, and melted very slowly. One tablespoon of dry mustard, a tablespoon of Worcestershire sauce, and a dash of cayenne pepper were mixed with a tablespoon of ale in a cup. As the cheese melted, the seasonings were added and stirred in, and then the ale was added very slowly as the mixture was being stirred constantly in one direction only. When everything had blended (be careful that the cheese never bubbles), it was poured over slices of toast, a dash of paprika added, and everyone fell to without delay. Of course, the beverage was cold ale, or beer.

One of the specialties of Savoie and Switzerland is a fondue made with butter, Swiss cheese, and white wine. It should be eaten from the chafing dish. Crusty French bread is served with it. Each guest breaks pieces from the bread, puts the piece of bread on a fork, and "dunks" the bread in the fondue, giving it a stir as he or she does so. This is a dish that is not only delightful and delectable, but one that you can have fun serving. There's nothing that breaks the ice at any party (outside of cocktails, of course) like everybody "dunking" in the same dish.

SWISS FONDUE

1 *lb. Swiss cheese, grated*	1 *cup very dry white wine*
3 *tbsp. flour*	*Salt*
Garlic	*Freshly ground pepper*
2 *tbsp. butter*	*Pinch nutmeg*
3 *tbsp. chopped chives*	2 *oz. kirsch*

Mix together 1 pound of Swiss cheese, grated, and 3 tablespoons of flour.

Put 2 tablespoons of butter in the top of a chafing dish, which has been lightly rubbed with a split clove of garlic. When the butter is hot, add 3 tablespoons of finely chopped chives, and sauté them for 1 minute. Then add 1 cup of very dry California white wine, and bring the liquid just up to the boiling point, but do not allow to boil. Keep it simmering and add the cheese and flour mixture slowly, and stir constantly in one direction until the cheese is melted. Continue to stir while adding salt and freshly ground pepper to taste and a pinch of nutmeg.

When the mixture starts to bubble (you're still stirring), add 2 ounces of kirsch (the Swiss Kirsch Dettling Superior Vieux, if you can get it), and when the kirsch has been added, serve immediately.

The Italians have a version of Cheese Dreams, which they call Mozzarella in Carrozza (in a carriage).

MOZZARELLA IN CARROZZA

8 *slices white bread*	¼ *tsp. salt*
Mozzarella cheese	1 *oz. dry white wine*
Flour	*Dash of Worcestershire*
2 *beaten eggs*	*sauce*
1 *cup olive oil*	

Cut off the crust from 8 slices of white bread, cut thin, and, as in Cheese Dreams, cut each slice in half. On each half slice of bread place a slice of Mozzarella the same size as the bread. Flour the whole thing well, and then dip in the lightly beaten eggs to which have been added the salt, dry white wine, and Worcestershire sauce. Fry the slices gently in about 1 cup of lard or olive oil, and serve very hot. Believe me, these items will go like hotcakes among any crowd of football rooters.

12. DESSERTS

The most popular school of thought on desserts holds that they round out and balance a meal, and that even an uninteresting meal, followed by an excellent dessert, is not a total loss.

Personally, I feel that a dinner is incomplete without the finale of a dessert, and that a dessert should have glamor, should create a stir of interest. In short, it should be spectacular.

Of all the desserts ever devised, none is more delicious, more effective, or swankier to serve than *Crêpes Suzette*. These glorified pancakes, so thin and delicate, combined with a rich *crêpe* butter and pungent liqueurs, have the most delectable flavor imaginable. Their final preparation at the table, with blue flames dancing above the chafing dish, brings an air of enchantment to the most simple setting.

CRÊPES SUZETTE

1½ cups sifted flour	¼ cup melted butter
¼ cup powdered sugar	2 tbsp. orange curaçao
Generous pinch salt	1 tsp. grated lemon rind
1 cup milk	5 eggs

Crêpe Butter

½ cup sweet butter
1 cup powdered sugar
Granted rind 1 orange

Granted rind 1 small lemon
½ cup orange juice
2 ounces yellow chartreuse

Crêpe Sauce

1 jigger Grand Marnier
1 jigger brandy
1 jigger kirsch

Combine in a mixing bowl 1½ cups of sifted flour, ¼ cup of powdered sugar, and a generous pinch of salt. Stir in slowly 1 cup of milk, ¼ cup of melted butter, 2 tablespoons of orange curaçao, and 1 teaspoon of grated lemon rind. Next add 5 well-beaten whole eggs, and beat the mixture vigorously until it is very smooth and of about the consistency of cream. Cover and let stand for about half an hour.

Grease a 5- or 7-inch skillet well with butter and when it is hot, put in enough batter to cover the bottom of the skillet with a thin layer (this will be about 2 or 3 tablespoons, depending on the size of the pan). Let the batter fry for a few seconds, then lift the pan from the flame and tilt it from side to side so that the cakes will be of uniform thickness. Cook until one side is brown (about 1 minute), then turn and fry the second side until brown. Take out the *crêpe,* roll up, and set aside. Continue this procedure until all the *crêpes* are made, keeping them warm.

To make the *crêpe* or Suzette butter, cream ½ cup of sweet butter in a bowl until light, then add 1 cup of powdered sugar, the grated rinds of 1 orange and 1 small lemon, ½ cup of orange juice, and 2 ounces of yellow chartreuse, poured in very slowly. Continue to beat until thoroughly blended.

For the final preparation, put a portion of the Suzette butter in a chafing dish, melting it over the low flame. Add as many of the rolled *crêpes* as the pan will comfortably hold, turn them so that they will heat through, then pour over them in the pan about a jigger each of Grand Marnier, kirsch, and brandy. Set them alight, and, tilting the top of the chafing dish from side to side, let the pan blaze for a moment. Then spoon out the *crêpes* and the liquid to individual plates. Repeat until all the *crêpes* are used.

Another of the greatest desserts ever devised by man is trifle. It is as English as Piccadilly, the Tower of London, and Buckingham Palace all rolled into one.

ENGLISH TRIFLE

1 *sponge cake*	*Macaroons*
Ladyfingers	*Raspberry jam*

1 *cup Madeira*

2 *cups milk*	¼ *tsp. salt*
6 *egg yolks*	*Grated rind ½ lemon*
½ *cup sugar*	2 *oz. brandy*

½ *tsp. vanilla extract*

½ *tsp. lemon extract*	2 *cups heavy whipping*
3 *tbsp. maraschino cordial*	*cream*
2 *tbsp. dry white wine*	*Sugar to taste*

Slivered almonds	*Candied cherries*

Line the sides of a glass bowl, or china salad bowl, with halved ladyfingers standing upright, the flat side of the ladyfingers resting against the sides of the bowl. Cover the bottom of the bowl with a 1½-inch layer of sponge cake, not too fresh. Spread a generous layer of raspberry jam over the sponge cake, and over the jam place a layer of macaroons. Pour over all 1 cup of Madeira— or enough to saturate the cake, macaroons, and ladyfingers thoroughly. Put in a cold place until wanted.
- Make a boiled custard, as follows: Scald 2 cups of milk. Combine 6 egg yolks, lightly beaten with ½ cup of sugar, the grated rind of ½ lemon, and ¼ teaspoon of salt. Slowly add the scalded milk to the egg mixture, stirring constantly. Put the whole into the top of a double boiler, and cook over hot water, stirring constantly, until

the mixture thickens and will coat a spoon. Cool, and add 2 ounces of brandy and ½ teaspoon of vanilla extract. Beat well, and set the custard in the refrigerator to chill.

In a glass bowl, which has been set in a larger bowl filled with cracked ice, mix together ½ teaspoon lemon extract, 3 tablespoons of maraschino cordial, 2 tablespoons of white wine, 2 cups of heavy whipping cream, and sugar to taste. Have the beater well chilled also. Whip the cream until stiff, then place in the refrigerator for a couple of hours.

To complete the trifle, pour the custard into the bowl containing the sponge cake, ladyfingers, and macaroons, put the whipped cream over the custard, building it up. Sprinkle slivered almonds over the whipped cream, decorate with candied cherries, and serve.

As I have confessed a number of times in the public prints, I can get along without most cakes very well. But a chocolate icebox cake is another story. That I go for in a big way.

CHOCOLATE ICEBOX CAKE

¾ lb. sweet chocolate	Ladyfingers
3 tbsp. sugar	Cream (sweet) sherry
3 tbsp. water	Slivered almonds
3 tbsp. Cointreau	1 cup whipping cream
6 egg yolks	Sugar
6 egg whites	Vanilla flavoring
Maraschino cherries	

Melt the sweet chocolate in the top of a double boiler, then add 3 tablespoons of sugar, the water, Cointreau (or orange curaçao), and the well-beaten egg yolks. Cook slowly until thick and smooth, stirring constantly. Then take the top out of the double boiler, and set it aside to allow the contents to cool. When it is cool, fold in the stiffly beaten whites of the eggs.

Line the sides and bottom of a medium-sized spring form cake pan with ladyfingers which have been split in

half lengthwise, putting the flat side of the split ladyfingers against the sides and bottom of the cake pan.
Moisten the ladyfingers with cream (sweet) sherry. Then
pour in half of the chocolate filling, and sprinkle the filling with slivered almonds (you can buy these in cel-
lophane packages). Then add another layer of split ladyfingers (flat side down) over the filling. Moisten them
with the cream sherry, and pour over them the balance
of the chocolate filling. Again sprinkle the top of the
filling with slivered almonds, and again cover the filling
with the split ladyfingers (flat side down), moistening
them with cream sherry. The total amount of cream
sherry needed will be anywhere from ½ to 1 cup. The
ladyfingers should not be moistened to the point where
they become soggy. Now set the cake, still in the spring
form cake pan, in the refrigerator for at least 12 hours
(you can make this the day before, and leave it in the
refrigerator until shortly before serving the next evening).

Shortly before serving time, remove the spring form
from the cake, leaving the cake on the bottom of the
pan. Cover the top generously with 1 cup of whipping
cream, whipped with a little sugar and a little vanilla
flavoring. Decorate the top with maraschino cherries,
and/or slivered almonds.

The famous French-born Sarah Bernhardt, was considered the greatest dramatic actress in America from
1880 to 1911. Talented, beautiful, accomplished at paint-
ing and sculpture in addition to the theater, Miss
Bernhardt was very much a part of the epicurean society
of her day. She often frequented Rector's, and her favorite
dessert, which she had difficulty in resisting, was
Charlotte Plombière, which is also known as Ginger
Crème.

CHARLOTTE PLOMBIÈRE

¾ cup sugar   1½ tsp. powdered ginger
⅛ tsp. salt   1½ cups heavy cream
4 egg yolks, beaten   3 tsp. kirsch
1½ cups scalded top milk   Ladyfingers

Combine the sugar, salt, and the beaten egg yolks. Then gradually stir in the scalded milk. Cook, over hot water, until of custard consistency, stirring constantly. Cool, and then stir in the powdered ginger. Turn into a freezing tray, and freeze until partially frozen, about 45 minutes. Turn into a chilled bowl, and beat quickly with a rotary beater until smooth. Fold in the whipped cream and the kirsch. Return to the freezing tray and freeze until partially frozen, stirring 2 or 3 times.

Line the bottom and sides of an 8-inch spring form pan with split ladyfingers. Spoon the partially frozen cream mixture into the pan. If you want to be real fancy, garnish the top with whipped cream put through a pastry tube. Place in the freezer compartment and freeze firm.

When ready to serve, remove the spring form pan. For an old-fashioned touch, the charlotte may be garnished with a red ribbon tied around the outside and a nosegay of flowers tucked into the bow! This recipe serves 8.

Fresh fruits are a great boon to harassed hosts and hostesses when they are stuck for a dessert. Any number of fruits can be combined in any number of ways with any number of wines and liqueurs, and the result is always tops. One could devote almost an entire book to fruits as desserts. I am going to limit myself in this chapter to only a few of the outstanding ones.

BING CHERRIES WITH BRANDY AND CURRANT JELLY

1 *lb. fresh Bing cherries*   4 *oz. red currant jelly*
                2 *oz. brandy*

Pit a pound of fresh Bing cherries and place them in a bowl with 4 ounces of red currant jelly. Mix, and then set in the refrigerator for several hours, until they are very cold. When you serve them, pour 2 ounces of brandy over the cherries and jelly. The brandy cuts the sweetness of the jelly, and the flavor of the whole is pretty wonderful.

Another exciting dish is Baked Bing Cheeries Flambéed.

BAKED BING CHERRIES FLAMBÉED

2 *cans pitted Bing cherries*   1 *grated lemon rind*
1 *tbsp. fresh lime juice*   1 *glass black currant jelly*
1 *grated orange rind*   *Slivered almonds*
                    4 *oz. kirsch*

Drain the Bing cherries thoroughly and place in a glass casserole. Pour over them the fresh lime juice, and sprinkle over them the grated orange and lemon rind. Cover with the contents of a glass jar of black currant jelly, and sprinkle slivered almonds liberally over the dish. Bake in a 375-degree oven for 10 to 15 minutes.

On serving, pour the warmed kirsch over the dish, ignite, and serve, flaming.

Here's a dessert that's swanky, suave, and swell, to say nothing of being simple. In any smart restaurant it will cost you anywhere from a dollar and a half to two dollars a copy, but you can make it in your own home at a fraction of the cost with canned cherries and you'll never know the difference.

CHERRIES JUBILEE

1 *large can Bing cherries*   3 *oz. Cointreau*
5 *oz. brandy*   3 *oz. kirsch*
                    Vanilla ice cream

Drain ¾ of the juice from a can of Bing cherries. Put the cherries and the remaining juice in a bowl, and add 3 ounces each of brandy, Cointreau, and kirsch. Allow the cherries to marinate in this mixture for a couple of hours.

Just before serving, warm the cherries and their marinade.

Serve out individual portions of vanilla ice cream in deep dishes. Put 2 ounces of brandy in a ladle, warm it, and set it alight, and with the blazing brandy ignite the cherries and their marinade. Mix while blazing, and ladle the cherries and their marinade over the ice cream.

Of all the desserts I have ever served, I have received more raves and more requests for the recipe for *Stuffed Peaches* than for any other. They're not so difficult to prepare as they appear to be.

STUFFED PEACHES

7 *ripe peaches*	½ *tbsp. chopped candied*
3 *macaroons*	*citron*
½ *tbsp. chopped candied*	2 *oz. curaçao*
orange peel	½ *cup dry white wine*
	1 *tbsp. brandy*

Select 7 peaches that are ripe, but firm. Cover with boiling water for 20 to 30 seconds, then drain, and cover with cold water. Remove, and the skins will slip off easily. Halve the peaches, and remove the pits.

Crumble 3 macaroons, and mix with them ½ tablespoon each of chopped candied orange peel and chopped candied citron, and 2 ounces of curaçao. Mash ½ peach to a pulp, and mix this with the crumbled macaroon mixture.

Pack the cavities of the peaches with the stuffing, and put each of the two halves together, securing them with toothpicks. Place the peaces in a baking dish, pour over them ½ cup of dry California white wine, and bake in a moderate (350-degree) oven for about 15 or 20 minutes, basting frequently with the white wine.

To serve, remove a peach to each plate, pour its share of the wine sauce over it. Warm a tablespoon of brandy, set it alight, and pour over the peach.

"Doubtless God could have made a better berry, but doubtless God never did," is the way Dr. Boteler characterized strawberries as reported by Izaak Walton in *The Compleat Angler*.

The French call strawberries *La petite reine des desserts*—the little queen of desserts. They prepare them in ways that will enhance their superb flavor, instead of overpowering them with too pronounced flavors. Typical are *Fraises Chantilly* and *Fraises Parisienne*. In the first the berries are cut in half and stirred into whipped cream sweetened and flavored with vanilla extract, or cordial. In the second whole strawberries are mixed with whipped cream and enough sweetened puree of strawberries to give a pink color. *Fraises aux Champagne* is a very elegant dessert—whole strawberries are sprinkled with sugar, chilled, then served in glass dishes with champagne poured over them.

Strawberry tarts have the same importance to the French as strawberry shortcake has to Americans. A baked pie shell or individual tart shells, made with rich pastry dough, is filled with either a custard, or rich creme, and is then topped with strawberries. The following is my favorite *Tarte aux Fraises*.

STRAWBERRY TARTS

Baked pie shell
3 tbsp. butter
1 tbsp. cornstarch
2 tbsp. flour
¼ cup sugar
1 cup milk

2 whole eggs
½ cup heavy cream
2 tbsp. kirsch
1 qt. fresh strawberries
3 tbsp. currant jelly
½ tsp. almond extract

2 tbsp. brandy

Melt 3 tablespoons of butter in top of double boiler and blend in 1 tablespoon of cornstarch, 2 tablespoons of flour, and ¼ cup of sugar until smooth. Add 1 cup of milk and cook over boiling water, stirring constantly, for 10 minutes. Add a small amount of the hot mixture to 2 well-beaten egg yolks, then add them to the hot mixture and cook 2 minutes longer, stirring constantly. Remove from heat and stir in ½ teaspoon of almond extract. Put top of double boiler into pan of cracked ice and stir the cream to cool it quickly. Then fold in 2 egg whites stiffly beaten, ½ cup of heavy cream, whipped, and 2 tablespoons of kirsch.

Turn the cream into a baked pie shell which has been

brushed with kirsch. Cover the filling with rows of whole ripe strawberries. Glaze the strawberries with 3 tablespoons of currant jelly melted and thinned with 2 tablespoons of brandy. Serves 5 to 6.

I have run across many recipes for Strawberries Romanoff, but they all failed to use the one ingredient which is typically Russian, namely vodka.

KLOOBNIKA ROMANOFF
(Strawberries Romanoff)

1 qt. strawberries	1½ oz. curaçao
½ cup powdered sugar	1½ oz. rum
1½ oz. vodka	1 cup whipping cream
	1 tbsp. kirsch

Wash and hull 1 quart of fresh strawberries, and toss them with about ½ cup of powdered sugar. Then put them in a bowl suitable for serving at the table, and pour over them a mixture of 1½ ounces each of vodka, curaçao, and rum. Place in the refrigerator to chill.

Serve very cold, with the strawberries topped with 1 cup of heavy cream whipped with 1 tablespoon of kirsch.

You don't need a grass skirt, a surf board, or a *lei* to concoct this delectable finale to a dinner. Just obtain a large pineapple—sun-ripened—and get out of your liquor closet a bottle of rum and a bottle of brandy.

BAKED PINEAPPLE

1 large pineapple	4 oz. light rum
½ cup blanched almonds	¼ cup sugar
1 large ripe peach	1 oz. brandy
	Butter

Cut off the top of a large, sun-ripened pineapple, saving the top for later use.

Scoop out the meat from the pineapple, using a curved grapefruit knife that is sharp, being very careful not to

puncture the skin of the pineapple. Discard any tough
or pithy meat, and cut the rest into about ½-inch cubes.

Shred ½ cup of blanched almonds and add to the pineapple meat.

Peel 1 large ripe peach, remove the pit, and cut into
pieces about the size of the pineapple cubes. Combine
the pineapple meat, the peach, and the almonds, and
pour over the mixed fruit 4 ounces of light rum. Sprinkle
with ¼ cup of sugar, and toss lightly.

Put the combined fruit back into the pineapple in
layers, dotting each layer with butter. Put the top of the
pineapple back on and bake in a moderate oven (350
degrees) until the inside fruit is tender.

Serve on a platter, pouring 1 ounce of warm brandy
over the pineapple, and setting it alight.

Another mighty good dessert is baked bananas topped
with coconut cream. Of course, bananas, coconut, and
rum go together like a "horse and carriage," or "love
and marriage," if I may borrow from an old popular
song.

BAKED BANANAS WITH COCONUT CREAM

6 *firm bananas*	1 *cup heavy cream*
Melted butter	2 *tbsp. sugar*
Brown sugar	1 *cup shredded coconut*
Rum	½ *tsp. kirsch*

Peel the bananas and arrange in a greased, shallow baking dish; brush with melted butter, sprinkle generously
with brown sugar, and drizzle a light rum over. Bake in a
375-degree oven for 15 to 20 minutes, or until the bananas are tender.

For the coconut cream, whip the heavy cream, sweeten
with the sugar, and fold in the shredded coconut, and
the kirsch. Serve this with the warm bananas. It will
serve 6 lightly.

I may be a little prejudiced, but I think my wife makes
about the best apple pie I have ever eaten. Some time ago

we concocted a plain old apple pie, but I added a touch to her apple pie recipe that raised it one notch to the best apple pie I will *ever* eat. Here is the recipe.

APPLEJACK APPLE PIE

Make your favorite pie crust, and put the bottom layer into an 8- or 9-inch pie pan or ovenproof pie plate. Meantime, have peeled and sliced fairly thin 5 cooking apples. Put a layer of sliced apples over the bottom crust, sprinkle over 3 tablespoons of sugar, a liberal sprinkling of ground cinnamon, and a liberal sprinkling of fresh lime juice.

Now comes the secret—sprinkle over the layer of apples ½ ounce of applejack, and liberally dot the whole with small pieces of butter. Then add another layer of apples, repeating the sprinklings of sugar, cinnamon, applejack, and butter, but omitting the lime juice. Then add another layer of apple slices, repeating with the sprinklings of sugar, cinnamon, applejack, lime juice, and butter. Put the top crust on, and bake in a 400-degree oven until the pie starts to cook. Then lower the temperature to 350-degrees, and continue to bake until the apples are tender, and the crust is brown (about 1 hour).

Applejack is another name for apple brandy, which the French call Calvados. It is one of the oldest distilled liquors known to mankind, and is strictly a natural liquor, with no other ingredient added—the distillation of the fermented juice of apples. So, naturally, it adds a piquancy to any apple dish.

This is another of my wife's superb pies.

FLORIDA LIME PIE

Prebaked pie shell	*1 can Eagle brand sweet-*
1 cup whipping cream	*ened condensed milk*
Sugar to taste	*⅓ cup fresh lime juice*
1 tbsp. rum	*3 eggs*

Mix together 1 can of Eagle brand sweetened condensed

milk, ⅓ cup of fresh lime juice, and the beaten yolks of 3 eggs. Then fold in the well-beaten whites. Place the mixture in a good, flaky pie shell, already baked, and bake in the oven for 10 minutes at 250 degrees. When cool, place in the refrigerator until ready to serve. When serving, top pie with slightly sweetened whipped cream to which has been added a little rum and sprinkle with powdered cinnamon. This recipe makes a pie that will serve six sparingly. But the odds are that four will finish the pie, because it's that good.

New England rum pie is one of those pies that men will probably take delight in making because it is impossible to have a failure with the crust.

NEW ENGLAND RUM PIE

Crust

⅓ cup sugar   18 graham crackers
Dash cinnamon   ¼ lb. butter

Filling

2 eggs   4 small pkgs. cream cheese
2 tbsp. rum   ½ cup sugar

Topping

1 cup sour cream   3 tbsp. sugar
                1 tbsp. sherry

Make a crust of 18 graham crackers, crumbled, ¼ pound of butter, melted, ⅓ cup of sugar, and a dash of cinnamon. Line a pie tin with this. For the filling, mix together 4 small packages of cream cheese, ½ cup of sugar, 2 beaten eggs, and 2 tablespoons of rum. When thick as cream, pour the filling into the crust and bake in a 375-degree oven for 20 minutes. In the meantime, mix together 1 cup of sour cream, 3 tablespoons of sugar, and a tablespoon of sherry. Spread this mix on the baked pie and cook 5 minutes more in the 375-degree oven. Chill before serving.

Down in the Deep South they make a pie of honey and nuts, and it really is something to write North about.

SOUTHERN HONEY AND NUT PIE.

3 tbsp. flour	1 cup milk
½ tsp. salt	1 cup chopped pecans
¾ cup honey	2 lightly beaten eggs
¼ cup orange curaçao	1 tbsp. melted butter
Cooked pastry shells	

Mix the flour, salt, honey, and orange curaçao, then add to this the milk and coarsely chopped pecans. Cook this in a double boiler until it is thick. Cool slightly, and add the lightly beaten eggs and the melted butter. Return the mixture to the double boiler and cook about 5 minutes, or until the egg is well blended and the mixture is not lumpy. Then pour into baked pastry shells, and bake in the oven long enough to reheat the pastry.

A variation of this honey pie is to put the filling into a 9-inch prebaked pie shell, and top with an apricot meringue. To make the apricot meringue, use 2 egg whites and ¼ cup of sugar, and 2 tablespoons of apricot brandy. Place in a moderate (350 degrees) oven to set, and delicately color the meringue.

There are certain festive occasions when you want your dinner to reach its climax with an elaborate dessert —in a blaze of glory, if I may coin a phrase! In such an event, there is nothing that can top a Baked Alaska.

People who have never had it sometimes refuse to believe that ice cream can be baked in the oven, and come out firm. But the ice cream is well insulated with sponge cake under it, and covered by a meringue. As a matter of fact, it is not at all difficult to prepare and serve at home, and it is much more fun than card tricks. You can get your sponge cake at your good neighborhood bakery, and your ice cream from your drugstore or the frozen food department of your favorite grocery store. All that you have to do is to make a meringue, assemble the various ingredients, pop it into an oven, and serve.

BAKED ALASKA

1 *qt. brick ice cream*	*Pinch salt*
Sponge cake, 1 inch thick	*½ cup Madeira wine*
4 to 5 egg whites	*Finely chopped cashew nuts*
½ cup powdered sugar	*4 empty eggshell halves*
1 tsp. orange curaçao.	*Warm brandy*

First get a hard-frozen brick of ice cream in any flavor you want. The most popular are tutti-frutti, vanilla, and strawberry. Tell your purveyor that you're going to make Baked Alaska, and you want it frozen especially hard, and packed in dry ice, so that it will remain hard-cold until you use it. Next you'll want a layer of sponge cake about 1 inch thick (or maybe 2 layers). This will be the base on which you'll put your ice-cream brick, and it should be an oblong piece that will project an inch all the way around the brick of ice cream. If 1 slice won't do, use 2, or trim to fit. You will also need a meat plank, or a small breadboard, and a sheet of heavy white paper.

Make the meringue, using 4 or 5 egg whites, about ½ cup of powdered sugar, 1 teaspoon of orange curaçao, or Cointreau, and a pinch of salt. Beat the egg whites in a chilled bowl until they are stiff enough to form peaks. Continue beating and add slowly the powdered sugar and the teaspoon of the curaçao or Cointreau. Set aside for a moment.

Now for the assembly job. Place the sheet of heavy white paper, trimmed to fit, over the plank or breadboard. On top of the paper place the platform of sponge cake. Sprinkle the sponge cake with Madeira wine, about ½ cup (the cake should not be soaked, merely moistened). On top of the cake place the brick of ice cream. Now, working fast, spread the meringue over the ice cream and cake, covering every bit of the ice cream and cake with at least a ½-inch layer of meringue, using a spatula. Sprinkle about a tablespoon of finely chopped cashew nuts over the meringue, and set in the top of the meringue 4 perfect eggshell halves. Now slide your masterpiece into a 450-degree oven (preheat the oven so that it is 450 degrees when you put the Alaska in) and let it brown lightly. It will take only a few minutes, and the meringue browns pretty fast. If you want to peek at the end of about 3 or 4 minutes, do so, but don't open the oven door wide, because a chill at the critical moment can collapse the meringue.

When browned, take the Alaska out of the oven, slide it onto a serving dish, fill the egg halves with warm brandy, set aflame, and serve quickly. And there you are!

A very grand and swanky dessert, yet simple to prepare, is a Champagne Parfait.

CHAMPAGNE PARFAIT

Fill tall parfait glasses ¾ full with pineapple or lemon sherbet or ice. With a glass stirring stick, about ¼ inch in diameter, drill a hole down the center of the firmly packed ice. Fill this hole with green crème de menthe. Then fill the glass with a good domestic champagne, and serve at once.

Zabaglione, the famous Italian dessert, is perfect at the conclusion of almost any dinner because it is light and most flavorsome. It is really a custard, but its consistency is such that you can almost drink it. The following recipe is the way Max Guggiari, of the Imperial House in Chicago, prepares it.

ZABAGLIONE GUGGIARI

5 *egg yolks*	9 *tsp. sugar*
5 *oz. Marsala*	1½ *oz. brandy*

In the bottom of a double boiler have the necessary

amount of water (to come within an inch of the bottom of the top part) at a temperature of between 90 and 100 degrees. Put the double boiler over a medium flame, and into the top part put the yolks of 5 eggs, 5 ounces of Marsala, 9 teaspoons of sugar, and 1½ ounces of brandy. With a wire whisk, whip this, without stopping, until the amount has increased to 4 times what it was at the start. Then pour into glass compotes and serve at once. The *Zabaglione* should be creamy, but just a little too thick to pour. Don't delay serving this dessert, because it will "fall" quickly and curdle if permitted to stand.

INDEX